Inclusion:
An Essential Guide
for the
Paraprofessional

A practical reference tool for all
paraprofessionals working in
inclusive settings

Peggy A. Hammeken

CORWIN PRESS
A SAGE Publications Company
Thousand Oaks, CA 91320

For information:

Corwin Press
A SAGE Company
2455 Teller Road
Thousand Oaks, California 91320
www.corwinpress.com

SAGE Ltd.
1 Oliver's Yard
55 City Road
London EC1Y 1SP
United Kingdom

SAGE India Pvt. Ltd.
B 1/I 1 Mohan Cooperative Industrial Area
Mathura Road, New Delhi 110 044
India

SAGE Asia-Pacific Pte. Ltd.
33 Pekin Street #02-01
Far East Square
Singapore 048763

Printed in the United States of America.

ISBN 1-890455-34-2

This book is printed on acid-free paper.

07   08   09   10   11   9   8   7   6   5   4   3   2   1

Table of Contents

Notes

"We grow because we struggle, we learn and overcome." -R. C. Allen

Introduction

The educational institution is an ever evolving entity. Some of the greatest educational changes in the recent history of education have occurred in the area of special education. Previous to 1975, the standards for educating students with disabilities varied greatly on a national scale. The majority of students with special needs received their education in separate classroom, special schools, or institutions, and some students received no formal education at all. The first major change for students with disabilities occurred in 1975 when the Education for All Handicapped Children Act (PL 94-142) was approved. With PL 94-142 the educational system was faced with the challenge of including all students with disabilities into the general education setting, as the law guaranteed a "free, appropriate public education" for all students. The law also mandated that, to the "maximum extent appropriate," children with disabilities should be educated with nondisabled peers in the "least restrictive environment." In 1997 the law was amended and became the Individuals with Disabilities Education Act (PL 105-17), commonly referred to as IDEA. Inclusive education has evolved and developed from this law.

In order to provide support and meet the needs of students in the general education setting, the reauthorization of IDEA in 1990 allowed for the use of paraprofessionals and assistants who are appropriately trained and supervised to provide support and related services to students with special needs. Without the support of trained paraprofessionals, it is very difficult, if not impossible, to include students with special needs and to meet their needs in the general education environment.

School districts across the country continue to struggle with the emergence of this educational system. With inclusive education, educators must expand their roles. Teaching no longer consists of one educator and a homogeneous group of students in the classroom. A typical classroom may have one general education teacher, a special education teacher, several paraprofessionals, and consultants working collaboratively to meet the needs of all students. The educators' new role also includes supervision of paraprofessionals, but educators frequently have not been trained as supervisors of adults.

IDEA clearly states that paraprofessionals should be appropriately trained and supervised, yet this training is often overlooked. So as you can see, inclusive education has brought about extensive changes in the educational system. Change is not always easy. It takes time, energy, and a belief that inclusive education is truly best for all students in order for the change to be successful.

With the movement towards more inclusive schools, new jobs for paraprofessionals have been created. In fact, the need for qualified paraprofessionals is in great demand and will continue to rise with the implementation of the *No Child Left Behind Act* signed by President Bush. At this time, the NCLB Act provides more control to local school districts on how the funds may be allocated. Many schools will spend a portion of this allocation on more formalized training for paraprofessionals since training is now required.

Nationwide, school districts are at various stages in the process of the implementation of inclusive programs. Some districts are in the initial stages. In these schools, the paraprofessional may be hired and expected to work with students immediately with little formal training. Be reassured that if you are in this situation, you will have a certified supervising teacher who will provide guidance and support, and this book will provide additional information to help you do your job more efficiently.

In contrast, school systems that have been involved with inclusive programming for a period of time may have extensive training programs in place for paraprofessionals. If you are employed in a district with a training program in place, this book will supplement your training and become a valuable reference tool. Although the book is not all-inclusive, it will provide both inexperienced and experienced paraprofessionals some supplementary information and a potpourri of ideas to help in working with students in the school setting. The majority of the ideas presented in this book have been collected and complied from the outstanding efforts of educators and paraprofessionals working in inclusive settings throughout the United States.

So whether you are about to pursue for your first job, have recently been hired by a school system, or are an experienced paraprofessional, this book will provide the support you need to make your job easier. If you are a special or general education teacher, this book is an important tool for facilitating the training of paraprofessionals within your school.

Inclusion: An Essential Guide for the Paraprofessional includes an overview of special education, basic guidelines to assist you when working in the educational environment, and an assortment of strategies and ideas to apply in the classroom environment. The book also includes various activities throughout the book. You may want to complete these activities alone or with a colleague and to discuss your responses with a supervising teacher. Appendix A includes reproducible forms to help you with various aspects of inclusive schooling and will help you to do your job more proficiently.

"The only person who loves a change is a wet baby."
- Ray Blitzer

Chapter 1

Building Background

The general education classroom, which includes all students with and without disabilities, is commonly referred to as the inclusive classroom. So what differentiates the inclusive classroom of today from the mainstream classroom of the past? In the inclusive classroom setting, all students share the same classroom space. Upon close observation, you will notice that some students may be completing assignments or carrying out activities that are completely different than those of their peers. A few students in the inclusive classroom may have an entirely separate goal. In the mainstream classrooms of the past, students with special needs were included into the classroom only when they were able to participate fully in the class activity. Therefore, students with special needs were often mainstreamed for classes such as music, physical education, recess, and lunch. In retrospect, these educational specialists (music, art and physical education teachers) have been including students and adapting and modifying their curriculum for many years. In today's inclusive communities, it is common to see students with and without disabilities playing together, working on projects together, and helping one another. In the inclusive classroom, students belong and are accepted as an integral part of the community.

Activities

Now take a moment to complete the following two activities. Although simple in nature, the purpose of these activities is to help you better understand some of the difficulties students have encountered in the previous dual education setting.

Activity #1 - Inclusion versus Exclusion

Inclusion! What does the word mean? Let's begin with the following simple exercise. Take a moment to recall an event during your childhood or teenage years when you belonged to a group and felt part of the community. Perhaps it was the band or orchestra, a club, a sports team, or a family event in which you participated. Now reflect about the feelings associated with the event. Think about how you felt when you participated in the group. Take a moment and write your feelings here:

Feelings When Included

_____
_____
_____
_____
_____

Now think about the word exclusion. At this time, call to mind an event from your childhood or teenage years when you were excluded from the group. Perhaps it was a bus ride when you sat alone, an activity or party to which you were not invited, or a family event when all of the attention was directed towards one of your siblings. Write your feelings associated with exclusion here.

Feelings When Excluded

_____
_____
_____
_____
_____

Now compare the two lists. Which list is longer? Usually the list pertaining to the "exclusion" part of the activity is longer. Powerful words such as lonely, misunderstood, rejected, depressed, or unhappy are frequently linked with the exclusion portion of the exercise. On the other hand, the words associated with the "inclusion" part of the activity help you to remember positive experiences.

From an early age, students have a strong desire to belong and be accepted by their peers. Students want to be a part of a group. Therefore, in order for a student to learn and be successful in school, the student must feel safe and accepted in the classroom environment. In order to be accepted and make friends, the student must be in the classroom.

Activity #2 - What Do I Do Now?

Let's consider another hypothetical situation. In the following situation, you an adult student enrolled a class at the local university. You arrive late to class and the professor has just finished a lecture. You slide into your seat and hope you haven't been noticed. On your desk is an assignment which you must complete. The professor asks all students to complete the assignment individually. Since you were not in the class for the lecture, you haven't the slightest idea what to do. What would you do? Write your choices here:

1. _____

2. _____

3. _____

4. _____

As an adult student, you have several choices. You may decide to set up an appointment with the professor to discuss the assignment, perhaps ask a colleague to help you out, or simply note on the paper that you arrived late and therefore cannot complete the assignment. As an adult, you are able to make these decisions. You will not be questioned and the professor more than likely will be lenient because you are an adult.

Now, let's change the hypothetical situation to involve an elementary level student. Imagine John, a sixth-grade student, is in a similar situation. John has just returned to his class from the resource room where he receives individual reading instruction in a supplemental reading series. (John is currently reading at a fourth-grade level.) The class has finished their reading lesson early and the students are working on an English assignment when John arrives. As John sits down, he glances at the English assignment. What options are available to John? List the options here:

1. _____

2. _____

3. _____

4. _____

Several options may include the following:

1. John tries to complete the English assignment without instruction.

2. John sits quietly until a peer or the teacher is available to assist.

3. John completes an unrelated assignment or project.

4. John disrupts the other students.

In the classroom environment, the four options listed above occur frequently. Upon examination, each option could possibly place John into a no-win situation. Let's examine why.

Option 1: John tries to complete the assignment without instruction. Students with disabilities often need extra time to complete assignments without appropriate modifications. In this situation, John not only missed the instruction, but is required to complete the assignment in less time. John may need support with both reading and writing; therefore, it may be very difficult for him to find the answers in a text or in another student's notes. It is unlikely that John will be able to complete the assignment on his own.

Option 2: John sits quietly until assistance is available. John has already transitioned to and from a special class. During the transition, approximately 10 minutes of actively engaged learning time is lost. This lost time includes transitioning to and from the special class and gathering or putting away materials in both settings. If John happened to meet a friend in the hall or stopped by the bathroom, the time could easily exceed 20 minutes. When John returns, he does not have sufficient background information to complete the assignment. With 25 or more students in the classroom setting, the teacher is unable to attend to John immediately. John needs to wait. Consequently, each transition may cost John 30 minutes of active learning time on a daily basis or 2 1/2 hours per week. If John leaves the classroom more than one time per day, the active learning time on a weekly basis is decreased substantially.

Option 3: John completes an unrelated assignment or project. This is a frequently used option. John may use the time to complete class work or work on projects. With this option there are several drawbacks and assumptions. Classmates notice John is not required to complete the same assignments. Therefore, an assumption may be made that John is unable to do the work. Classmates may feel it is unfair that he does not have to complete the work. These assumptions may isolate him from his peer group. They may have a negative impact on his self esteem.

Option 4: John disrupts other students. John returns to class with no available support. No appropriate assignment is available so John begins to talk to or disrupt other students. John is reprimanded by his teacher.

Please note that in the previous options, a crucial question was not addressed. If John is required to do the assignment, when will he find the time? Will John need to complete the assignment as homework? During recess? If John does not complete this assignment, will he be able to do the next English assignment or is this assignment a prerequisite to the next lesson?

It is very difficult for a student to be successful in the classroom setting while working within a fragmented educational program. In a dual educational system, students who often require the most consistency in programming often receive the least. The student must manage two curriculums, two classrooms, two teachers (or more), and, frequently, two sets of rules.

In the inclusive classroom setting, the student remains in the classroom for instruction and the assignments are often modified to meet the student's individual needs. The student does not lose valuable learning time transitioning between classes or waiting for assistance upon return. The general education teacher has more flexibility as the teacher does not have to wait until a student returns from a pullout session to begin a new lesson. Lesson times can be monitored and adjusted immediately, increasing the actively engaged learning time for all students.

Inclusive Practices: Myth and Reality

Inclusive programs do not all look the same. The federal law provides the framework for schools, but the law is often interpreted differently throughout the country. This interpretation causes confusion between states, districts, and even individual schools.

There are many myths related to inclusive education. Here are some of the most common:

Myth: General education students receive a "watered down" curriculum to compensate for students with special needs in the classroom.

Reality: This is one that is heard frequently. The general education curriculum is adapted and modified to meet the specific needs of the individual student. These changes have no effect on the general education curriculum. Adaptations and modifications may include alternate forms of testing, extra class time to complete assignments, reading materials aloud to students, or adjusting the goals and objectives for individual students. These changes virtually have no impact on the curriculum for the other students.

Myth: All students with disabilities must complete each assignment in the same manner as the students in the general education classroom.

Reality: The students' assignments are based on the Individualized Education Plan (IEP). The assignments may be modified or adapted for the student if necessary.

Myth: Students are placed into the general education class without support and assistance.

Reality: In a well organized inclusive education program, paraprofessionals and special education teachers provide support to the general education teacher. This may be in the form of consultation, adaptations, modifications, team teaching, and/or trained paraprofessionals providing assistance under the direction of the supervising teacher in the classroom setting.

Myth: Inclusion is not beneficial for the general education students.

Reality: As school populations become more diverse, curriculum and materials are adapted, modified, or changed for students with special needs. These adaptations may also be used to accommodate students experiencing similar difficulties, for at-risk students, and also for Title I students. The students in the classroom setting often are exposed to sign language, Braille, communication boards, medical devices, or special equipment. Students learn at an early age that all children have the same thoughts and feelings, regardless of their limitations. Most important, students learn that they are more alike than different. A strong sense of community develops within the classroom environment.

The inclusive setting is unique to the school system for which it is developed. An inclusive setting does not just occur naturally. The groundwork is actually in place before the student enters the classroom. Numerous students experience success in the classroom environment with the support of paraprofessionals, and it would be very difficult for students to be included in the classroom without the additional support. The added support (even though intended for the student with special needs) helps all students. With an extra adult in the classroom, there is further opportunity for individualized instruction; student progress is more easily monitored. As well as providing additional academic support, the paraprofessional is also a positive role model for students.

For a small percentage of students, alternate forms of placement are needed. In inclusive settings, a continuum of services is available. The continuum of services for students with IEPs ranges from a fully integrated setting (fulltime in the general education classroom) to a segregated setting, such as a residential center. Alternate placement must be available for students who are unable to make academic gains after assistance and modifications to the curriculum or environment have been implemented in the general education setting. Therefore, paraprofessionals may work with students in many capacities either in the classroom or in an alternative setting.

Benefits of Inclusive Education

Think about the negative feelings generated in the exclusion portion of the previous exercise in this chapter. For the majority of students with special needs, inclusion helps to increase the student's self esteem. No longer is the student removed from the classroom to attend a special class, with a special teacher, in a special room. The student views the classroom setting as a safe place to participate and take risks, which are necessary to learn and succeed.

- Inclusive education supports the current educational system. In the general education classroom, modifications and strategies directed toward students with disabilities are beneficial to the general education students as well. The strategies and modifications help to improve and individualize the existing curriculum for all students. These modifications and strategies become a part of the general education teacher's files and may be used in the future for students with similar academic needs.

- Inclusive education encourages effective collaboration. No longer is the educational system divided into two separate systems. The educational system is united. This is beneficial because:

  Communication and collaboration increase as the new educational team is formed.

  No individual is expected to have all the expertise required to meet the educational needs of students in the classroom.

  When team members with knowledge in many diverse areas work together in cooperative problem-solving, results are achieved more quickly.

- Inclusive education improves the quality of onsite training. Instead of providing separate inservice for specific disabilities or modification strategies, the educational team learns together. All inservice relates directly to the individual student. The training is relevant because all members of the team have accepted ownership for the student. Team members learn by doing.

- Inclusive education has benefits for all students. When two adults (or more) work collaboratively in the classroom, questions are answered more quickly, projects are easily monitored, and all students receive more individualized attention. Students accept one another as contributing members of the school community.

Inclusive education currently is and will continue to be a controversial issue in the field of education. Large amounts of time and energy are expended in the debate over whether or not inclusive education is best for students. In the meantime, students with special needs are in the classrooms and they need your support. These students have a desire to learn, to be accepted, and to be successful. It is the job of the educational team to provide the most appropriate educational setting, given the resources which are available within the individual school districts.

Notes

"The great thing in this world is not so much where we stand,
but what direction we are moving."
- Oliver Wendell Holmes

Chapter 2

The Special Education Department

Welcome to the world of special education! The term special education broadly defines the multiple educational programs designed to serve children with disabilities. As a paraprofessional, you are a member of the special education team, which consists of professionals with expertise in many specialized areas. All special education departments operate under a due process of law system. State and federal laws must be adhered to. In order to work within the system, it is important to be familiar with some general information in relation to the special education department. This chapter describes the process of placement, the use of labels, the roles of multidisciplinary team members, and, briefly, your role in relation to members of the team.

Student Placement

In order for a student to receive special education services, a multidisciplinary team must determine if the student meets specific criteria and is eligible to receive service. The team is commonly referred to as a multidisciplinary team because each team member has a specialized area of proficiency. A student is usually referred to this team by the classroom teacher and often in conjunction with the parent because the student is not progressing as expected in the classroom environment. Once the referral is made, the parent receives a written notification from the school. If a decision is made to assess the student, a signed written permission form is needed from the parent or guardian before the assessment can begin. Once the signed permission is received, the special education process begins. The student is then assessed by the various members of the team. The assessment may include the use of informal assessments, standardized tests, and classroom observations. When all of the assessments are complete, the team members reconvene to compile the data and determine whether or not the student qualifies for special education services. If a student qualifies for special education service, an Individual Education Plan (IEP) is written. The IEP is a legal document which summarizes all of the assessment findings, records specific student needs, and lists the criteria necessary to assist the student with meeting the goals outlined in the IEP. Classroom accommodations and modification strategies are defined. The student's Individual Education Plan is written based on the student's needs, not the handicapping condition. Once an IEP is written, the school is obligated to provide the services it details. The IEP is reviewed biannually and rewritten annually. A complete reassessment occurs every three years.

Handicapping Conditions

Paraprofessionals new to the field often have questions related to the student's handicapping condition. The handicapping condition may also commonly be referred to as area of exceptionality or identified disability. The most frequently asked questions by those new to the field often include: "What is the identified handicapping condition?," "what is the difference between the handicapping conditions?," and "how should students be served in relation to this disability?"

The purpose of this section is to define some commonly used terminology and provide a general explanation of the various handicapping conditions. Special education is not a science, but guidelines do exist for placement and the guidelines must be adhered to. Characteristics between the various handicapping conditions listed will often overlap as there is no typical student with a specific learning disability, behavior disorder, language impairment, or other handicapping condition.

Students who are identified for special education often need accommodations to compensate for their various exceptionalities. These accommodations provide support to the student and are only a small part of the student as a whole person. Frequently when people refer to students with disabilities, the focus is placed on the disability even though the disability is only a small part of the student. Let's look at a very simple example. If you use prescription glasses, you have vision which is correctable with the use of glasses. The glasses are used to accommodate for the low vision and allow you to see well. In view of the fact that low vision is easily corrected, you would not qualify for special education services. However, if prescription glasses had not been invented, you would need accommodations in order to function. The accommodation which makes a difference in your life is the use of prescription glasses. For many students, there is a fine line between whether they qualify for special education services or not. For some of the students who qualify, simple accommodations may also make the difference of whether they are able to function in the classroom. Therefore, it is important to remember that a disability is only a small part of the person, and many students with appropriate accommodations are able to function very well. When referring to students with special needs "person first" terminology is used. If you need to refer to a student with a disability, the correct terminology is "a student with learning disability," "a student with a behavior disorder," "a student with a low vision," "a student who uses a wheelchair," and so forth.

There are currently twelve areas of exceptionality in the federal law. Since the language often varies between states, the following chart lists the terminology stated in the federal law followed by common terminology frequently used by individual states. For example, in one state, "PI" may stand for a student with a physical impairment, whereas in another state, it may refer to a student with a perceptual impairment. If you would like additional information regarding definitions and criteria, you are encouraged to contact the special education department or the Department of Education in your state.

Federal Terminology	Common Terminology
Autism	Autism
Deaf-Blind	Deaf-Blindness
Hard of Hearing	Hearing Impairment (HI) Hearing Impaired (HI)
Mentally Retarded	Cognitive Delay (CD) Developmental Delay (DD) Mental Handicap (MH) Mildly-Impaired (MI), Severely-Impaired (SI)
Multihandicapped	Multiple Disabilities
Orthopedically Impaired	Orthopedic Impairments
Other health Impaired	Other health Impairments
Seriously Emotionally Disturbed	Behavior Disordered (BD) Conduct Disorder Socially Maladjusted
Specific Learning Disability	Learning Disability (LD) Learning Differences (LD)
Speech Impaired	Speech and Language Impaired (SL)
Traumatic Brain Injury	Traumatic Brain Injury (TBI)
Visually Handicapped	Visual Impairment (VI)

At the present time, there is discussion at the federal level related to adding Attention Deficit Hyperactivity Disorder (ADHD) as a disability category. Currently students with ADHD do not qualify for special education services unless, in addition to the diagnosis of ADD, they meet the criteria for one of the categories listed in the previous chart. Some states will provide service to students under "other health impaired" or write a 504 Plan. With a 504 Plan the student may receive additional support through general education.

It is very important to be aware that labels are primarily used as an identification tool. Once the student is placed in a special education program the label is secondary. In fact for many students will not be aware with their handicapping condition unless you ask or read the student's Individual Education Plan.

Autism

Autism is a developmental disability that occurs during infancy or early childhood. It is behaviorally defined syndrome characterized by an uneven developmental profile. Autism ranges from mild to severe. Many students with a mild form of autism do very well in the school setting. This developmental disability significantly affects verbal and nonverbal communication and social interaction. Some of the characteristics of autism include irregularities and impairments in communication, engagement in repetitive activities and movements, resistance to change, and unusual responses to sensory experiences. Asperger's Syndrome is considered a mild form of autism.

Deaf-Blind

Students identified as deaf-blind have a combination of hearing and visual impairments. This combination often causes severe communication and other developmental and educational problems. Due to the complexity of the disability, this student is not able to be served solely under the category of hard of hearing or visually handicapped.

Hard of Hearing

Students identified as having a hearing impairment lack the ability to hear sounds and discern clarity. The hearing loss may range from a slight hearing loss to deafness. For many students, the impairment is so severe that the student is impaired in processing linguistic information through hearing, with or without amplifications which adversely affects development or educational performance. The hearing impairment has no effect on the student's cognitive ability. Some mild hearing disorders are not identified until the student enters school. Many students are identified by their general education teacher. A hearing loss may become apparent as the student frequently turns his head to one side and asks to have the volume raised on audiocassette players, filmstrips, and movies. It may be difficult for the student to follow oral directions. Directions may need to be repeated frequently. Poor articulation skills are often apparent as the student may be unable to hear the sounds well enough to reproduce them. In addition to service from the specialist for the hearing impaired, the student frequently receives support in the areas of speech and language.

Mental Retardation

The degree of impairment for students with mental retardation determines whether the student is considered mildly, moderate, or severely impaired. A student with a mild to moderate impairment has below average cognitive ability and therefore, learns at a slower rate than his peer group. Functional skills also lag behind those of their peers. Students who are mildly mentally retarded will learn to read, write, and perform basic math, although these skills will take longer to acquire. A large discrepancy exists not only in the acquisition of academic tasks, but also in the student's growth both socially and emotionally. Students may have trouble paying attention, generalizing skills, applying previously learned skills to new situations, remembering information, using language, or thinking abstractly. Due to difficulty in learning, some students have low self esteem or poor self-concept. The student usually requires large amounts of repetition to learn skills presented in the classroom. Some characteristics are similar to those of a student with a learning disability, but a major difference does exist. The LD student has definite strengths and limitations with learning, whereas, the student with a mild impairment is below average in all academic areas. Functional and social skills usually lag behind the skills of their peer group.

Some students' IQs may fall in the area of severe and profound. These students experience extreme difficulty with academic learning. Students in this category may have unique physical needs. Some students will exhibit behaviors such as tantrums, outbursts, and aggressive or passive behavior. Educational programs assist students with learning appropriate social behavior, self help skills (which include personal care or grooming), communication, functional academic skills, and to develop independent living skills.

Multihandicapped

Students identified in this area have a combination of disabilities such as mental retardation and visually handicapped or mental retardation and orthopedically impaired which adversely affect the student's development. Since these students have several handicapping conditions often the student cannot be served solely under one handicapping condition.

Orthopedically Impaired

Students identified in this area have a severe orthopedic impairment which adversely affects the development or educational performance. The term includes impairments caused by congenital anomaly, as well as impairments caused by disease and from other causes.

Other Health Impaired

Students identified in this area have limited strength, vitality, or alertness, due to chronic or acute health problems such as a heart condition, asthma, epilepsy, leukemia, diabetes, epilepsy, spina bifida, cerebral palsy, or amputations which adversely affects the students' development or performance. This category is very broad. Along with the physical and medical needs, some students have a secondary handicap such as a learning disability, communication disorder, or severe impairment. Due to the uniqueness of each handicap, these must be defined individually. Cognitive abilities range from below average to superior. Some students may have multiple handicaps or are confined to a wheelchair. Others require no special education service, with the exception of nursing services. Some students are absent frequently, due to extensive medical care. The service provided by the special education department varies depending upon the student's IEP. The special education department will provide information to you regarding these low incidence handicaps.

Seriously Emotionally Disturbed

Some students are identified as seriously emotionally disturbed. Terminology, again, varies from state to state. Some states refer to students as emotionally disturbed, conduct disordered, or socially maladjusted. Students in this category must exhibit specific behaviors over a long period of time and to a marked degree. Behaviors must interfere with the student's educational performance in the classroom and cannot be explained by intellectual, sensory, or health factors. Some characteristics may include the inability to build or maintain relationships with peers and teachers, inappropriate feelings under normal circumstances, depression, or a tendency to develop physical symptoms or fears associated with personal or school problems. Attention-seeking behaviors such as hitting, fighting, and destruction of property may be apparent. The student may be hyperactive, withdrawn, or depressed. Consistency in programming, definite limits, and expectations must be clearly defined for these students.

Specific Learning Disability

The largest group of students identified to receive special education support receives service under the category of a specific learning disability. Students with a learning disability have average to above average intelligence, but for some reason are not achieving in one or more areas at their perceived ability. In order for a student to qualify for a learning disability many states also require documentation of processing. Processing refers to the manner in which the brain receives, stores, and outputs information. Everything a person sees, hears, smells, touches, or tastes is stored within the brain. To recall information, the brain must be able to sort and retrieve the information. When educators speak about processing, they are referring to this process. For students with a learning disability, this process interferes with the ability to learn. Some feel the documentation of processing helps to distinguish an LD student from a student who is underachieving.

For the LD student, difficulties may be apparent in the areas of reading, language arts, math, or language. Difficulties may occur in isolated areas or be evident across several areas of the curriculum. Expressive (speaking) or receptive (understanding) language can affect reading or the general acquisition of information. For others, visual discrimination of shapes, letters, and symbols is demanding. This makes copying from the board, reading, or writing difficult. Auditory processing is also common. Difficulties in this area include the ability to follow multi-step directions, discriminate between sounds, or express themselves verbally. Students may experience difficulty with fine and gross motor skills. Fine motor skills include writing, cutting, pasting, drawing, and holding a pencil. The large or gross motor skills include walking, running, catching or kicking a ball, or skipping. Another area that may impact the student's ability to learn is behavior. Some students are hyperactive, unable to focus, unable to stay on task, or unable to follow classroom routines. Social skills may also be inadequate. A severe discrepancy between the students' cognitive (intellectual) ability and their academic performance must be documented. This information is obtained during the initial assessment. The majority of students with a learning disability have average to above average cognitive ability, but fail to perform at an academic level which commensurate with their perceived ability.

The profile of a student with a learning disability will exhibit definite strengths and limitations in various academic areas. For example, the LD student may excel in math, yet struggle with reading and written language. The student may read fluently, yet not comprehend the material due to difficulty in the acquisition of language. The student may have strong verbal skills and dominate classroom discussions, yet be unable to write a simple sentence.

This term does not include children who have learning problems which are primarily the result of visual, hearing, or motor disabilities. Also excluded are children with mental handicaps, behavioral disorders, or difficulty learning as a result of environmental, cultural, or economic situations.

Speech Impaired

Many students identified in special education receive services for speech and language. A language impairment can be in the area of expressive (speaking) or receptive (understanding) language, or the student may experience a language delay. To qualify for special education service, the impairment must impact the student's performance in the classroom. Students who experience difficulty with receptive language often have difficulty understanding directions or oral presentations. Grammar, sentence structure, and vocabulary support are often required.

Deficits in the area of expressive language may include articulation (substituting, omitting, distorting, or adding sounds) and fluency (stuttering) disorders. Some students are unable to organize their thoughts and ideas. Spoken language may be rapid and disorganized. Students with expressive language difficulty often feel uncomfortable participating in classroom discussions.

Voice disorders also fall under the umbrella of speech and language disorders. Voice disorders relate to the pitch, sound, or quality of the sounds produced.

Traumatic Brain Injury

The student identified as TBI has an injury to the brain (or head) caused by an external physical force or an injury caused by a stroke or aneurysm resulting in total or partial functional disability which affects educational performance. The term includes open or closed head injuries resulting in mild, moderate, or severe impairments in one or more areas. Some of the areas of deficits may include language, memory, attention, sensory, perceptual and motor abilities, physical functions, and information processing to name a few.

Visually Handicapped

The student identified as visually handicapped has a visual impairment which, even with correction, adversely affects a child's development or educational performance. This term includes both partially seeing and blind students. Some students have low vision. With low vision, the student may be able to see materials and objects that are close, but unable to see the blackboard, overhead, or distant objects. Another area is often referred to as visually limited. A visually limited student may need special devices such as special lighting or magnifiers. Special equipment is provided by the vision teacher. Because of low vision mobility is a concern for some students. Large and small motor development may also be delayed. Depending upon the degree of the impairment, modifications and supplemental devices are provided in the classroom environment.

ADD/ADHD and Gifted and Talented

There are several additional areas which may or may not be served in the area of special education. Since the following are not listed by the federal mandate, they are noted separately.

Two areas which receive a great deal of attention are the areas of Attention Deficit Disorder (ADD) and Attention Deficit Hyperactivity Disorder (ADHD). At this time these areas are not listed as a handicapping condition by the federal government. The diagnosis for ADD and ADHD is determined by a medical doctor outside of the school setting. Students diagnosed with ADD/ADHD are served under the umbrella of special education only if they have been diagnosed with a handicapping condition, such as a specific learning disability. The student is then provided service under the handicapping condition of specific learning disability.

Since ADD/ADHD is not listed as one of the twelve preceding handicapping conditions, it is important to note it here. Some common characteristics of students with ADD may include difficulty paying attention and remaining focused over a long period of time, consistent carelessness with daily assignments, inattentiveness during class, repeated misplacing of materials and supplies, incessant blurting out of answers, difficulty waiting his turn, and frequent disrupting in the classroom. Many of these students are easily distracted and forgetful in classroom settings. Students with ADD who are also hyperactive (ADHD) may also fidget or talk excessively or have trouble remaining seated. It is important to note that many of these characteristics will apply to numerous students in the classroom and that all students who exhibit these characteristics are not automatically ADD or ADHD.

Students who are gifted and talented (GT) may be served in the area of special education if they have a secondary handicap which is part of the federal mandate. Gifted students are often overlooked for special education services because they are frequently able to compensate for the disability during their educational careers. Students who are gifted and talented will not meet the criteria for service if they are able to achieve at or above grade level. Periodically you may work cooperatively with the GT department if a student has a secondary diagnosis of a specific learning disability or a behavior disorder.

As mentioned earlier, in order to qualify to receive service under the umbrella of special education, students must be assessed and meet specific criteria. The identification process is lengthy and comprehensive. Many students are referred to the special education team for assessment each year. Of the students assessed, many do not meet the predetermined qualifications and, therefore, do not qualify for special education service. The students who do meet the criteria are placed into special education.

"Never doubt that a small group of thoughtful committed people can change the world; indeed, it's the only thing that ever has."
-Margaret Mead

Chapter 3

The Multidisciplinary Team

As a paraprofessional, you may have little or no experience working within a school setting. For some of you, this may be the first time you have entered a public school since your high school graduation. A number of you may have volunteered in your children's classrooms, chaperoned field trips, and helped teachers with various projects throughout the school year. A few of you may have children with special needs and be very familiar with the special education system.

The special education system is continually changing. The special education department is very different from the classroom environment, as the entire department functions as one very large team. All major decisions become team decisions, the student's program is developed by a team, and the services are provided as a team. You are a part of this team and your main responsibility as a paraprofessional will be to help students by providing support under the direction of this team.

The students who receive support under the umbrella of special education receive service from a team which is often referred to as the multidisciplinary team. The team consists of many members, and the members change depending upon the unique needs of each student. Special education team members have different licensures. Some may be licensed to teach students with mental retardation, others may be certified to teach learning disabilities and so forth. With the multidisciplinary team, all teachers are able to provide support to all students with special needs as long as at least one person on the team has the appropriate licensure. If the person with the licensure is unable to directly serve the student, this professional becomes a consultant for the other team members. Minimally, the members of the multidisciplinary team consist of the psychologist, the special education teacher, the classroom teacher, a parent or guardian, and an administrator. Listed below, in alphabetical order, are the staff members who may be part of the multidisciplinary team.

Administrator
Adaptive physical education teacher
English-as-a-second language teacher
General education teacher
Hearing impaired teacher
Nurse or health assistant
Occupational therapist
Paraprofessional
Parent
Physical therapist
Psychologist
Social worker
Speech and language clinician
Special education teacher
Vision teacher
Vocational educator

The following section is written to help increase your understanding of the multidisciplinary team members. The first paragraph describes the member's role on the team. The second part includes comments related to the possible relationship which may occur between the paraprofessional and the team member. There is space at the end of each description for you to add information and comments specific to your individual situation.

Administrator

The school administrator is a member of every educational team. The administrator makes administrative decisions, provides assistance with student schedules, coordinates inservice for staff, and provides support in the development of inclusive settings. The administrator creates the positive environment necessary for successful inclusion.

The school administrator oversees the entire special education department. Due to the size of the special education department, most administrators will have one contact person. The special education contact person is often referred to as the "lead teacher." If you have questions, the questions should be directed first to the lead teacher, who will convey the information to the administrator if needed. If you have specific questions or concerns which you would like to express to the administrator, it is best to discuss the issue with the lead teacher first, and, if the problem cannot be solved, follow the proper channels in the department before setting up an appointment with the administrator. Some administrators have an "open-door" policy and welcome comments and concerns to be expressed directly.

_____

_____

_____

_____

English-as-a-Second Language Teacher

The English-as-a-second language teacher (ESL) assists students whose primary language is other than English. The main role of the ESL teacher on the multidisciplinary team is to assist with the assessment of students who do not speak English.

If an ESL student is placed in special education, the ESL teacher will consult with you and provide appropriate modifications in conjunction with the special and general education teachers.

_____

_____

_____

_____

General Education Teacher

The general education teacher usually initiates the special education referral to the special education department either alone or in conjunction with a parent. The teacher has a wealth of valuable information regarding the academic progress and the social-emotional well-being of the student. Information regarding the student's organizational skill, work habits, processing of information, and language is also contributed by the general education teacher. Once this information is compiled, a team decision is made on whether or not to proceed with the assessment. The classroom teacher's information also helps to determine which specific areas should be assessed.

In an inclusive setting, a close relationship develops with the general education teacher. More frequently than not, you will be working in the classroom under the guidance of the general education teacher. The classroom teacher will set the rules, guidelines, and expectations for the classroom. The expectations will be different for each classroom in which you work. The instruction for the students may be provided by the general or special education teacher. Your role in the classroom will vary depending upon what has been documented in the IEP and on the unique needs of the individual student. It may include behavior management, reteaching or reinforcing skills, working with students in small groups, reinforcing self-help skills, assisting with mobility, and carrying out the modifications provided by the general and special education teachers.

_____

_____

_____

_____

_____

_____

_____

Hearing Teacher

This teacher is responsible for the assessment of students with hearing impairments. Hearing losses may range from mild to severe. The role of this specialist is to check hearing aids and adaptive devices and to provide direct instruction or consultation to the classroom teacher. Some students may require the services of a sign language interpreter.

The hearing specialist will provide inservice, direct instruction, and assist with strategies and ideas to accommodate the student within the classroom environment. If you work directly with this student, you may be required to learn how to use various adaptive devices in the classroom and provide support academic support to the student.

_____

_____

_____

_____

Nurse or Health Assistant

The school nurse screens students for vision and hearing, offers explanations of medical records and conditions, monitors prescription medicine, teaches specific health care skills, checks fit, maintenance and function of prosthetic and adaptive devices, and assists parents with medical referrals.

You may be involved with the school nurse or health assistant daily if a student takes medication, requires daily medical attention, or uses prosthetic and adaptive devices. If a student has an emergency medical plan, the school nurse will be able to clarify the procedures for you.

_____

_____

_____

_____

Parent or Guardian

The parent or guardian is involved in each step of the educational process. To place a student in special education, a signature must be obtained. The parent or guardian provides invaluable information relative to their child's strengths and limitations. Information relating to health, social or emotional levels, and other pertinent data contributes to the development of an appropriate educational program.

The supervising teacher will define your role in relation to the parent. You may be responsible for keeping a daily notebook to share with the parent. This notebook might include a daily activity update, a log of homework assignments, general comments regarding the day, or comments about the student's behavior. The special education teacher will tell you what and how to report these items. You may also be asked to communicate with the parent by telephone on a regular basis.

_____

_____

_____

_____

Physical and Occupational Therapists

The physical therapist focuses on the assessment, training, and use of the lower extremities and large muscles. The occupational therapist focuses on the upper extremities and fine motor abilities.

Both therapists will offer suggestions for modification and the adaptation of materials. Special equipment may be provided, and in the majority of cases, you will be trained in the use of these devices. Recommendations regarding the general classroom environment and suggestions for student accommodations will also be provided to you. As a paraprofessional, you may be spending large amounts of time with the student and your observations are important to this professional.

_____

_____

_____

_____

Psychologist

The school psychologist's expertise is in the administration and interpretation of standardized tests. The cognitive ability tests (intellectual functioning tests) are administered and scored by the school psychologist. In addition, observation of students, family history, and compilation of student data may be completed by the psychologist. The psychologist is able to assist with the design and implementation of interventions and behavior management systems. The school psychologist also acts as a resource for the building staff.

The school psychologist may contact you for your observations regarding individual students. Feel free to contact the psychologist for information about child development, learning styles, or recommended reading materials on specific disabilities.

_____

_____

_____

_____

Social Worker

The social worker acts as a liaison between the home, the school, and community agencies. The social worker may counsel students and families, assess the effects of a student's home life on school performance and assist families in emergency situations. The social worker often is able to contribute valuable information regarding the student's social and emotional well-being that may impact the student's ability to learn.

You may be contacted by the social worker for observations regarding specific students. If a student shares information with you regarding his or her safety, well-being, or family situations that may be harmful to the student, it should be reported immediately to the social worker, supervising teacher, or administrator.

_____

_____

_____

_____

Special Education Teacher

The special education teacher is responsible for academic testing and student observations. When a student qualifies for placement, the special education teacher oversees the implementation of the student's program. Each special education teacher is responsible for a specific group of students and is commonly referred to as the case manager of the particular group. The manner in which students are divided depends upon the individual school district. Some districts divide students by handicapping condition. In this case, teachers with a degree in learning disabilities only serve students who have been diagnosed with a learning disability. Teachers with a degree in the area of mildly impaired serve only students labeled as such. Other districts use a multidisciplinary team approach, allowing all special education teachers to work directly with all students, as long as one member of the team holds the appropriate licensure and acts as a consultant.

The special education teacher is the first person with whom you will have contact. You may work with one or several special education teachers throughout the school day. Their role is to define your job and provide basic guidelines and expectations for the individual student. They will develop the appropriate adaptations and modifications, which you may be responsible for implementing. The special education teacher is responsible for seeing that the student's Individualized Education Plan (IEP) is adhered to. Questions regarding the student's program should be directed to the special education teacher responsible for the specific student. If your questions are unable to be answered, you will be referred to another member of the team.

_____
_____
_____
_____

Speech and Language Clinician

The speech and language clinician determines whether or not language impacts the student's learning in the classroom environment. The clinician's main role on the multidisciplinary team is to assess students for speech and language disorders. Once the student is in the program, the clinician works with the student to remediate articulation, voice and fluency disorders, or language (both expressive and receptive) difficulties.

The speech and language clinician assists with fostering communication skills in the general classroom environment. Supplemental materials and specific exercises to be implemented within the general education setting often will be provided and you may be responsible for implementing them. The clinician will also provide ideas and materials for the reinforcement of language skills.

_____
_____
_____
_____

Vision Teacher

The vision teacher assesses and provides information for the student with vision impairment. Vision impairments may range from low vision to legal blindness.

The vision teacher often supplies enlargements, audiocassettes, large-print books, materials in Braille, and inservice, if needed. If you have a student with a visual impairment in the general classroom, you will work closely with the vision teacher or consultant.

_____
_____
_____
_____

Vocational Educator

The vocational educator provides valuable information regarding the student's work and career potential. The vocational educator offers job counseling, exposure to various jobs, assistance with job placement, and coaching on the job. The vocational educator is employed at the secondary level.

Under the direction of the vocational educator, you may assist students with the acquisition of skills necessary for job placement. You may also be responsible to monitor, provide support, or oversee a student on the actual job site.

_____
_____
_____
_____

Additional Staff Members

There may be additional staff members with whom you work. Use the following additional space to include any pertinent information you would like to list.

_____
_____
_____
_____
_____
_____
_____
_____

During the first few weeks of employment, you may want to complete Form #1 located in Appendix A. On this form, list the people with whom you have frequent contact. Include the individual name, position, contact information, and perhaps a brief note to help you remember specific important information.

Notes

"By constant self-discipline and self-control you can develop a greatness of character."
-Grenville Kleiser

Chapter 4

Confidentiality

As a paraprofessional, you will establish a relationship with teachers, school personnel, students, parents, and the community. The quality of your relationships depends not only on the work you perform, but also on the ethical behavior you demonstrate on the job. Ethics are particularly important because, as a paraprofessional, you are placed in a position of authority over students. You may encounter situations when your interests, the student's interests, and the school's interests are in conflict. In a situation such as this, the best interest of the individual student should always be considered first.

One of the most important aspects of ethical behavior is handling confidential information related to students. The privacy rights of all students and their families must be respected. During the course of a school day, you will receive information and perhaps overhear comments about family situations, behavioral issues, test scores, or other personal information. All of this information is confidential and must not be shared beyond the family and/or the educational team. If this information is shared, it can only be shared when directly relevant to the student's education. Such discussions related to students should also take place in a private location. Both state and federal laws regulate access to information related to students with disabilities. As a paraprofessional, you are also required to uphold the ethics of confidentiality.

The following information provides some very simple answers to some very complex legal issues. This section has been included to increase awareness of the legal issues that affect students and staff members. The information is not intended as legal advice but is intended to provide some guidelines. Questions should be directed to the special education department.

IEP (Individualized Education Plan)

All documents pertaining to the student and the student's program are confidential and it is important that the confidentiality be respected. The IEP includes information relevant to the student's performance in the areas of academics, communication skills, adaptive functioning skills, vocational assessment, and sensory, health, social, and emotional areas. Psychological testing may also be included in this file. The IEP is written annually and are updated throughout the year. Therefore, this file not only includes the current information but all of the previous IEPs. Since the documents are a part of the student's permanent file, the special education file is placed in a separate folder within the cumulative file. If this file is removed from the general file, a log sheet must be signed and dated, and the reason for viewing the file must be documented. (The special education department will provide you with the proper procedure for your district.) Some special education departments encourage paraprofessionals to read the files, whereas other departments prefer to verbally share only the pertinent information that will help to improve the working relationship between the paraprofessional and the student.

Individualized Education Planning Meetings

You may be asked periodically to attend IEP meetings. At these meetings you may also be asked to share information regarding the student's performance in the classroom environment. On occasion, personal information is shared by the parent(s) that will help the staff better understand the student. Often this information (such as a separation, a pending divorce, financial difficulties etc.) is not documented into the IEP. It is important to note that all information shared during an IEP meeting or any parent meeting is confidential.

The Special Education Department

The special education department is a department full of activity. Many school districts do not have the luxury of private conference rooms, so conversations and meetings may be held in the special education area. Frequently, conversations and consultations take place between team members. Members may include social workers, psychologists, school nurses and outside consultants. All comments and conversations are confidential and should not be discussed with others.

The General Education Classroom

General education teachers are accustomed to working alone in the classroom setting for the greater part of the day. Not all teachers are comfortable with another adult in the classroom. Relationships are built on trust and mutual respect. It will take time to establish a relationship with the classroom teacher, and the easiest way to damage the relationship is to criticize or discuss the supervising teacher with others. Your role is to support the special education students in the classroom. Do not discuss specific classroom or student situations which occur with others.

As a paraprofessional, you may be assigned to a grade level or specific department. There may be times when you observe a specific teaching technique or a unit that may benefit others who are teaching the same subject matter. If this is the case, write down the information and ask if you may share the information or suggest that the teacher share the information at an upcoming department meeting.

In addition to the adults, you will develop a relationship with the students in the classroom. If you have knowledge that a student in the classroom is being abused or neglected, you are required to report this information to your supervising teacher.

Parents

As a paraprofessional, you will have frequent contact with parents in both the school setting and the community. It is important to remember confidentiality also applies outside of the school environment.

In the past, lawsuits have been initiated on behalf of students due to breach of confidentiality. The best way to avoid any such confrontation is to honor confidentiality for every student. For this reason, conversations regarding specific students must be confined to the school setting and occur only with adults directly involved with the student.

You should avoid sharing information about a student's progress with the parents or guardians unless you have been provided with specific directions by the supervising teacher. If a parent asks questions about a student's IEP or other legal issues, ask them to contact the special education department.

Special Education Students

Students in the classroom regularly have questions regarding their peers with special needs. At the elementary level there are many books which will explain the various disabilities in caring and compassionate ways. These books can be read aloud to the class. Disability awareness books can easily be found by searching online or inquiring in the school media center.

At the elementary level you may be asked some of the following questions. You may want to discuss these questions with the special education staff and determine some appropriate responses based on the grade level in which you work. Possible responses have not been listed as the responses are numerous and the answers depend upon the age of the student asking the question.

"How come John gets all of the easy work?"
"Why does Vanessa talk to funny? I can't understand her."
"Why does Kaman use a wheelchair, hearing aid.......?"
"What's wrong with Roberto?"
"How come you have to go to the bathroom with Natalie?"

Often, if a student has a severe disability the school nurse, special education teacher, or the parent will provide general information about the disability to the entire classroom. This allows the students to ask questions and have their questions answered. At the middle school and high school level, some students feel comfortable with their disability and are able to explain and answer questions on their own.

Students will look to the adults in the classroom for examples about how to interact with students. As an adult, it is important to model patience, tolerance, and acceptance. Students will learn from your example. When students ask direct questions it is important to remember to respect the rights and privacy of the student when answering. It is also important to emphasize to students that they are more alike than different.

Activities

Activities #1 and #2 include two hypothetical situations. In each case, read the paragraph and then answer the question. Some possible responses are listed at the end of each activity. When you have completed the activity, you may want to discuss your response with your supervising teacher. Form # 2 in Appendix A includes additional discussion activities with space to write in your response.

Activity #1 – The Teachers' Lounge
Ms. Allen is a paraprofessional who works in a second grade classroom. She spends the majority of her day with Josh, a student who has behavior problems and reacts strongly to change. Earlier that morning, Ms. Allen has been told that Josh's parents have just separated. During lunch, Josh explodes. He throws his lunch tray at Ms. Allen and yells, "I hate you as much as I hate my parents."

When the incident is over and Josh has calmed down, Ms. Allen joins a group of colleagues for lunch. Much to her surprise, Josh is the topic of their conversation. Ms. Allen does not comment and quietly eats her lunch. As she prepares to leave, one of her colleagues asks her what is going on and if it's true that the Josh's parents have separated. If you were Ms. Allen, what would you do?

_____

_____

_____

_____

_____

_____

Possible Response: When Ms. Allen realized her colleagues were discussing Josh, she should have explained immediately that it is a breach of confidentiality to discuss the student. No response is often construed as support. When asked by her colleagues about the separation an appropriate response would be that she is unable to discuss the student's family life. The incident should be documented and given to the student's supervising teacher.

Activity #2 – In the Community
Mr. James is a paraprofessional at a middle school. After school he is employed as a trainer in the weight room at the local athletic club. A parent of one of his students works out in the weight room every afternoon and they have become friends. He repeatedly asks Mr. James about his son's progress in school. If you were Mr. James, how would you respond?

_____

_____

_____

_____

_____

_____

_____

_____

Possible Response: This can be a difficult situation as Mr. James works directly with the student and is an acquaintance of the parent. One response is to provide general positive information such as he is working very hard, he is a great kid, etc. If the parent persists with questioning Mr. James can ask the parent to set up an appointment with the classroom teacher and say that he would be very happy to attend also. He may also explain that he does not like to discuss any student outside of the school setting.

It is important to remember that you are a professional and that professionals honor confidentiality in all settings. It is not only out of respect for the student and family that the emphasis is placed on confidentiality; it is also the law. As an employee of a school district, you always need to respect the privacy and confidentiality of your co-workers, your students, and your students' families.

Guidelines for Confidentiality

Do not discuss students in a public place. If discussing your job with friends, do not use students' names or provide specific information that may identify students, families or coworkers.

Do not offer information if you are not sure whether or not it should be considered confidential. When in doubt, it is best to say nothing. Simply state that you cannot answer that question or refer the person to the special education teacher.

Do not share information with anyone not directly related to the student.

Do not keep personal notes or files on individual students. If you must keep this information, it should be in a folder and, if possible, placed in a file cabinet or other secure location.

Do not remove personal files without following the proper procedure.

Do not discuss staff members, department issues, or student issues with any school-based personnel if they are not directly involved in the situation

Notes

"Choose a job you love and you will never have to work a day in your life."
-Confucius

Chapter 5

Getting Started

The paraprofessional's job can be very demanding, but it is also very rewarding. Demonstrating a positive attitude (especially during a difficult time) is important when working with students. Your attitude is contagious to those around you. When you are positive, students and staff with whom you interact are more likely to be positive.

Paraprofessionals play an important role in providing service to students with special needs. The additional support you provide in the classroom (or special education area) helps to provide additional learning opportunities and more individualized instruction for all students.

The Paraprofessional's Role

Your role is determined by the student's unique needs and also the needs of the special education department. You may work in a classroom environment with several students, be assigned to support an individual student throughout the day, or work in a separate setting such as a resource room.

As a paraprofessional, your job is to support and assist students within the classroom. The Individualized Education Plan (IEP) provides the framework. The supervising special or general education teacher will provide assistance and guide you as you provide support to individuals or small groups of students. The supervising teacher is responsible for the direct instruction of students, whereas your role includes the reinforcement or reteaching of skills, behavior management, and curriculum support for the special education students. Your job may also include lifting, personal care, or assisting students with mobility. Due to the uniqueness of each student, the job description of every paraprofessional is unique. Some examples of your role may include but are not limited to:

- creating individualized learning materials and modifying existing curriculum materials

- providing remedial instruction and reinforcement skills

- assisting students with individual or group activities

- helping students with make-up work

- assisting students with interpreting and following directions

- reinforcing skills that have been previously taught

- administering tests individually

- monitoring and providing assistance to students during seatwork activities

- supporting students with daily assignments (in all areas)

- reading aloud to individuals or small groups, or providing support for independent reading

- assisting with organizational skills

- checking for work completion or homework

- playing educational games

- assisting with behavior modification strategies

- assisting with lifting and rotating students

- assisting with personal hygiene, including feeding and diapering

- keeping records documenting behavior of individual students

- maintaining daily logs or journals

- communicating with parents regarding homework or daily activities

- communicating with general education and special education teachers

- assisting students with motor or mobility limitations

- performing routine office duties such as typing, filing, taking messages, or photo-copying materials

- supervising of students during lunch or recess and when getting on/off the bus

The previous list includes some of the duties that you may be asked to perform. The responsibilities vary depending upon the students served and the type of support needed to enhance the educational program. Shown below is a partial sample of Form #3 located in Appendix A. This form should be filled out in conjunction with the special education teacher. The supervising teacher will list the responsibilities, and then collabo-ratively it will be determined whether or not follow-up training is needed. If training is needed, it should be documented where and when the training will take place. As you are assigned to classrooms this form may be used to list the specific responsibilities for each individual classroom.

Form 3 Sample - General Responsibilities

Paraprofessional Responsibility	Training Needed	Follow-Up Date
Reinforce skills taught by the general education teacher		
Monitor daily homework assignments		
Assist students with organizational skills		
Administer individual tests		
Implement teacher-designed materials with individual or small groups of students		
Assist student with motor or mobility limitations	X	prior to working with student
Supervise student during lunch and recess		
Assist student with personal care	X	prior to working with student

Role Delineation

There is a clear delineation of roles between the supervising teacher and the paraprofessional. In the classroom environment, there are some responsibilities which should not be assigned to paraprofessionals. For example, the paraprofessional should not be solely responsible for the classroom if the supervising teacher is absent, nor is the paraprofessional responsible for creating lesson plans or providing the initial instruction to students. As a paraprofessional, you may reteach and provide reinforcement, but you should not be providing the initial instruction. Following are some comparisons of roles in various situations.

Form #4 Sample - Roles and Responsibilities

Educator	Paraprofessional
Plans the weekly lesson plans	Reinforces the lessons under the guidance of the supervising teacher
Determines the objective for the lesson	Provides support to students to help meet the lesson objective
Provides initial instruction for the class	Reinforces the lesson and provides drill and practice activities
Assigns silent reading activity to entire class	Reads materials aloud to an individual or a small group of students
Administers essay test to all students	Writes the answers that student dictates
Develops with student and parent a specific plan for daily homework completion	Monitors the daily homework plan with the student
Implements medical schedules with nurse or nursing assistant	Accompanies the student (if necessary) to health room to accommodate medical needs
Plans and initiates conferences with parents	Participates in the conference, if appropriate
Implements behavior plan and determines consequences for student	Monitors and documents information on the daily plan

A copy of Form #4 is also included in Appendix A and may be used for documentation purposes only. This form is useful if you encounter times during a classroom activity when you are unsure of how to do what you have been asked to or if you question whether or not it is your responsibility. You may use the Form #4 to document the teacher activity, the paraprofessional activity, or both. At a later time you may follow-up with the supervising teacher.

Developing a Schedule

Once your job description is outlined and defined, a schedule will be prepared. The schedule is developed collaboratively with the special and general education teachers. You may rotate between classes, be assigned to one classroom, or spend small amounts of time in several classrooms. Perhaps your schedule will include support in a computer class for one student, a physical education class with another, and lunch with a third. Each paraprofessional's schedule will be different due to the unique needs of each student. The following schedule has been developed for a paraprofessional who works in multiple classrooms throughout the day.

Form #5 Sample – Daily Schedule

Daily Schedule

Time	Location	Activity	Case Manager
9:30 - 9:40	Classroom #1 Room 200	Pick up student from bus	P.C.
9:45 - 10:00	Classroom #2 Room 206	Homework completion Daily schedule overview	H.P.
10:05 - 11:00	Classroom #3 Room 108	Language Arts - Reteach - Read aloud with students	P.C.
11:00 - 12:00	Gym Room 131 Room 132	Mon. - Phy. Ed. Tues. – Art Class Wed. – Computer Class Monitor student behavior during class	L.S.
12:00 - 12:30	Break	Lunch	
12:30 - 1:10	Lunchroom	Lunchroom and playground duty	P.C.
1:10 - 1:30	Prep time Consultation		
1:30 - 2:00	Classroom #2 Room 206	Reading block	K.R.
2:00 - 3:00	Classroom #4 Room 110	Math class Drill and reinforcement Supplemental curriculum provided by special ed. teacher.	P.C & H.R.

Form #5 in Appendix A is a blank copy of the Daily Schedule. Transfer your daily schedule to this form. Note that on the sample schedule, students' names are not listed. If you would like to list the students, consider using initials in case the schedule is misplaced. Once it is complete, use the schedule for several days. Note any areas that do not seem to be effective. For example, you may find that the time allowed for transition between classes is insufficient, attending to medical needs may take longer than originally anticipated, or the classroom schedules may change. The schedule needs to be revised until it is effective. It is not uncommon to make schedule adjustments over a period of several weeks.

If you are scheduled into classrooms, there will be times when classroom instruction is taking place and you may feel you as though your time is wasted. This time is important and valuable for several reasons. It allows you time to observe the student(s) in the classroom setting. During these observation times, write ideas that will provide support to the student(s) with the lesson. During this time, you may also take notes or write key vocabulary words, main ideas or questions that can be reinforced when the direct instruction is complete. You may also use this time to note specific observations about the student's behavior, update communication logs, or work on curriculum modifications. This time is valuable for the general education teacher as well. The teacher will be able to monitor and adjust the assignment, deviate from the lesson plan if needed, or terminate the lesson early without providing an individual explanation to you at a later time.

Scheduling for a Substitute

As soon as your schedule is created, you must prepare a folder for a substitute paraprofessional in case of your absence. Since your job varies and you work with many teachers, a substitute folder is essential. If you work with a student with specific medical or personal needs, it is important to train a colleague to act as a back-up for you. Discuss this with the special education teacher. The substitute folder should include your personal schedule, a contact person in case the substitute has questions or needs clarification, and a map of the school with emergency exits and classrooms highlighted. If applicable you may also want to include some of the following:

Bus duty. If your responsibility includes support to students entering and leaving school, list the students, their bus numbers, and approximate time of pick up and delivery to the bus. Include any special instructions. Pictures of individual student(s) are helpful for the substitute, especially if the substitute is required to meet the student in the morning.

Special medical or personal concerns. You may be responsible for reminding students about medication times. List the student, classroom, and time for the student reminder or for escorting the student to the health room. Some students may have feeding tubes or catheters. List the student and the time the student is to be taken to the nurse. When working with toilet training, list student's name and bathroom breaks or changing times.

Classroom duties. When providing academic assistance in the classroom, list the class, time, room number, and name of the general and special education teachers. List the first names of the students you are responsible for overseeing and, if appropriate, write general comments regarding each student. Some students experience difficulty with transitions and changes in routine. If you anticipate an adverse reaction to a substitute from a specific student, discuss the situation with the general education teacher. The general education teacher may be able to provide program consistency while you are absent. Many times, changes occur in the daily classroom curriculum. You will not be aware of these. The general education teacher will guide the substitute when you are absent. If there are emergency medical plans or alternative behavior plans for specific students, attach a copy to your schedule.

Lunchroom. If you attend lunch with a specific student, provide the name of the student, and the reason for attending lunch (student needs support in the lunch line, student has a tendency to choke, student needs help with outerwear) on the substitute plan.

The substitute folder is very important and should be completed in advance. Bus duty, lunchroom, and medical concerns should be written clearly and concisely. If your school has a map it is helpful to highlight the classrooms in which you provide support and also the emergency exits. It is also important to list the name of a colleague who will be able to answer any questions the substitute may have. Make copies for the special and general education teachers.

Effective Communication Strategies

Paraprofessionals are a valuable asset to the classroom, and most teachers welcome the support that you provide. Working together in a team situation requires frequent and open communication.

Effective communication is a critical and complex skill which is often taken for granted. It is often assumed that everyone communicates effectively, although this is often not the case.

One component of effective communication is speaking. It is important to speak clearly so others can easily understand what you are saying. When providing information to colleagues either verbally or in a written form, it is important to report the specific observations and try to be as objective as possible. Describe what you have seen or heard, but avoid drawing conclusions. It is important to establish a common vocabulary. The use of technical language by educators often isolates the paraprofessional from the conversation. When working together, the special and general educator should make every attempt to teach and explain the language and specific terminology used. You in turn should also attempt to learn some of the common terminology and acronyms which are frequently used in education. If there are terms which are consistently used that you do not understand, write the terms down and ask at a later time.

The second component of communication is listening. To be an active listener, you need to focus on what the person is saying. If you do not understand, do not be afraid to ask the speaker to clarify the intent. If a direction is not clear, paraphrase it; do not hesitate to ask questions when you need clarification. It is not uncommon to think one knows exactly what is going to be said before the speaker has finished. Often when this happens a listener begins to anticipate his turn to speak and may mentally rehearse a response, thereby missing part of what the speaker has actually said.

The following tips will help you to communicate more effectively and develop a positive role in working with teachers.

- Think before you speak.

- Listen well enough to ask related questions about the topic.

- Put as much energy into listening to others as you do when speaking to others.

- Paraphrase what you understand others to be saying.

- Observe what times of the day are best for individual interactions.

- Ask "how" and not "why."

- Avoid using words such as "always" and "never."

- Use "I" statements.

- Observe others who speak and note the qualities you admire. Select some of these qualities and try to incorporate them when you are speaking or listening.

As a paraprofessional, it is imperative to develop effective communication skills. You will be working with many different teachers, colleagues, and parents. The book Collaborative Practices for Educators-Strategies for Effective Communication by Patty Lee, Ed.D., is listed in Appendix B, the resource section of this publication. This small book is an excellent resource which can help you increase both speaking and listening skills.

Written communication is another important aspect of your job. You will be responsible for reporting to the special education teacher regarding student performance in the classroom. With your insight, the special and general education teachers will continue to review and revise overall plans for the student. There are several methods of reporting and providing feedback information to your supervising teacher. Daily, weekly, and monthly meetings may occur.

Daily Communication

If you are assigned to one or several classrooms, finding time to discuss issues and concerns and clarifying lessons or activities on a daily basis is essential for a well-run program. It is important to schedule a specific time to meet each morning and to honor this time period. A daily five-minute conversation with the classroom teacher (before the students arrive) will help the day to progress efficiently. At times, the supervising teacher will need to make changes to lesson plans or modify the daily schedule due to unforeseen circumstance. It is important that you are aware of these changes as they will also affect your schedule.

If you are in the classroom, you will also need to communicate frequently with the supervising special education teacher. Some days you may speak with the special education teacher directly, whereas other days you may need to provide information in a written format. Therefore, you may want to document information in a daily log. A sample of Form #6 has been completed as a model. Appendix A includes a reproducible copy of Form #6. This form may be used for an individual student or it may be used for the entire day as in the sample. Form #7 in Appendix A provides an additional form which may be used.

Form #6 Sample – Daily Log

DAILY LOG
Student: Dana   **Date: Feb. 3**   M **T** W TH F
9:30 Dana was able to remove outerwear with the assistance of a peer (third time this week). He prefers to have peer help instead of assistance from an adult.
Student: Sharon   **Date: Feb. 3**   M **T** W TH F
10:00 Sharon is unable to keep up with the daily science assignments. She is struggling with the reading and becoming frustrated. Should the assignments be read aloud? Modified in length? Or the requirements for the number of assignments be modified?
Student: John   **Date: Feb. 3**   M **T** W TH F
12:00 Ms. Johnson received a telephone call from the transportation office regarding John on the bus. Please see her ASAP.
Student: Mary   **Date: Feb. 3**   M **T** W TH F
1:00 Mary has been asked to leave the art class twice this week for hitting, poking, and disrupting the class. Please see the art teacher before the next art class, which is Tuesday of next week.
Student: Susan   **Date: Feb. 3**   M **T** W TH F
2:00 Math class is running smoothly. Susan is participating more with the problem-solving activities. She has completed the alternate curriculum and I will need more supplemental curriculum by Tuesday morning. Thanks, Mary Johnson

When completing a Daily Log, write the observations objectively. Always include the student's name, the time, the day, and the setting. As a paraprofessional, you may work with the student for only a small portion of the day. The special education teacher is responsible for the student's entire program. The information on this simple log provides information which helps the special education teacher piece together the student's entire program. From the simple comments on the form, the special education teacher may conclude the following information:

During the 9:30 time block, it was noted that Dana was able to remove his coat (for the third time) with peer support. This is important as it indicates that Dana is becoming more independent and asking for assistance from a friend instead of depending upon an adult. If a goal on Dana's IEP is to become more independent and take care of removing his outerwear without the help of the paraprofessional. Dana may be moving toward meeting this objective by asking a peer to help with the task he is unable to complete alone.

At 10:00, it was noted that Sharon has been experiencing difficulty in science. This note may indicate to the special education teacher that the curriculum is becoming too difficult or that perhaps the science vocabulary and the reading level is too high in this specific textbook. Perhaps she will need additional support in this class. Another question that may arise is whether or not she is having difficulty with reading in other academic areas or whether she is only experiencing difficulty with the science textbook.

At 12:00, the general education teacher received a telephone call from the transportation department regarding Jim. Due to privacy there are no details listed on the form. If this were extremely urgent, a telephone call would have been placed to the special education teacher instead of asking for a meeting. Therefore this note indicates that the special education teacher will need to follow up.

At 1:00, Mary has been asked for the second time to leave class. Since it seems this is unusual for Mary, several questions may arise. Is Mary only acting out during this class? Is she experiencing difficulty in the class with her peers or is something happening at home that the school is unaware of at this time?

At 2:00, Susan needs additional supplemental materials that are provided by the special education teacher. In this case, the paraprofessional is asking for additional materials with several days of anticipation. The special education teacher can determine whether Susan's work is too easy, whether she is ready to move on to another level, or whether or not Susan is able to participate more in the general education curriculum.

This form may be used for all areas of the curriculum. In addition to reporting the areas of difficulty, it is also essential to list the areas where the student has experienced success. This will help the team adjust the curriculum based on the strength areas. For students who experience difficulties in the area of behavior, a daily communication log helps to identify specific areas of concern. Often, difficult students tend to be disruptive at specific times or only during certain class periods. This valuable information should be given to the special education teacher so that modifications to the curriculum or environment can be made for the student. Due to confidentiality, fold or put the form into an envelope for the special education teacher. If time permits set aside five to ten minutes per day to meet with the special education teacher. During this time, you can share your direct observations about the student. If there is an area of immediate concern, you will need to set up a meeting to explain the situation.

As the team develops, you will be able to cover more information during the allotted time period. When meeting with the special education teacher keep in mind that each special education teacher is often responsible for supervising several paraprofessionals in addition to working with students, so conversations should emphasize the most important areas. It is a good idea to make a list of items you would like to discuss prior to any meetings.

Prior to working with individual students, specific concerns should be discussed, and alternate plans (if needed) should be in place. Students with severe behavior problems and those with special medical concerns must have a back-up plan in place. These plans should be updated frequently. It is imperative to anticipate a problem and be prepared to handle it, instead of discovering during an emergency that no plan is in place. For the majority of students, the plan is rarely implemented, but if you do need to use it, it will be in place and you will be prepared. Following, you will see two sample forms. The Back-Up Discipline Plan (Form #8 Sample) and should be filled out by the special education team. This form is used for students who may be unable to follow the classroom rules, students who are consistently disruptive in the classroom, and students with severe behavior problems.

Form #8 Sample – Back-Up Discipline Plan

Back-Up Discipline Plan
Student's Name: _____ Date:_____
Special Education Contact: _____
General Education Contact: _____
Back-Up Discipline Plan:
_____
_____
_____
Additional Information:
_____
_____
_____
If assistance is needed, please call the following person(s).
Contact Person with Telephone Number
☐   Administrator   _____
☐   General Education   _____
☐   Special Education   _____
☐   Paraprofessional   _____
☐   Parent   _____
☐   _____   _____
☐   _____   _____
☐   _____   _____

The Medical Alert Form (Form #9 Sample) should be filled out by the nurse at the beginning of the school year. You must have a clear understanding of the exact procedures to follow should an emergency situation arise. Form #9 Sample is an example of a form which may be used for students with specific medical concerns. If you work directly with the student, you will need to be aware of the specific medical needs and the exact procedure to follow in case of a medical emergency. The Medical Alert Form #9 located in Appendix A may be reproduced and used for students with allergies or those prone to seizures, choking, or malfunction of various medical devices.

Form #9 Sample – Medical Alert Form

Medical Alert Form

Student's name: _____

Special Education Contact: _____

General Education Contact: _____

☐　**This is an emergency situation. Call 911 immediately and then contact the following people.**

Contact Person   Telephone Number
1. _____
2. _____
3. _____
4. _____

Notes: _____
_____
_____

Area of Concern: _____

Symptoms: _____
_____
_____

Additional Information:
_____
_____

If assistance is needed with this student, please call the following people.
Contact Person and Telephone Number
1. _____
2. _____
3. _____
4. _____

Copies
☐　General Education
☐　Special Education
☐　Nurse
☐　Paraprofessional
☐　Parent
☐　_____
☐　_____
☐　_____
☐　_____

If you assist a student with mobility, a school map that highlights the various emergency evacuation routes which are handicapped accessible should also be attached to the map.

Both of the preceding forms should be kept in a file where you have immediate access to them. All professionals who are involved with the student should also receive a copies. If there is a situation where a medical or behavior plan needs to be implemented, the special education teacher should be contacted immediately. Do not wait until the end of the day.

Weekly Communication

You will consistently be taking notes and writing observations regarding the students with whom you work. Some departments schedule a weekly meeting to discuss general concerns related to students. The notes and, perhaps, the Daily Log information can be discussed at this time.

If the general education teacher provides a copy of the weekly lesson plans, the lessons plans may also be discussed at this time. Modifications for the upcoming week will be planned jointly or provided for you by the supervising teacher. Once you know the student(s) and the expectations of the general education teacher, many of the modifications and adaptations will remain consistent and you will be able to create them on your own.

Monthly Communication

Monthly meetings may be used to look over upcoming units, set long- and short-term goals, and develop curriculum modifications. Do not save daily observations or questionable issues regarding individual students for monthly meetings. These observations must be shared daily or weekly.

Observations

As an employee, you may also be observed during student contact time. Some school districts may require one or two observations per calendar year. Observations provide positive comments about your skills and interaction with the students. Some school districts require yearly long-term goals. These goals may be written in conjunction with the general and special education teacher, or you may write them on your own. An example of some goals may include:

Increase communication with special and general education teachers

Attend a class in relation to a specific disability

Become proficient in the use of specific adaptive devices

Try one new technique with a specific student per week

Keep a list of successful modifications for a specific student

Attend a CPR course

The special and general education teachers may be able to offer additional suggestions about your specific goals and may suggest areas for improvement.

Breakdown in Communication

There are times when a breakdown in communication may occur. Inevitably, when people work together, they have different ideas of how things should be done. It is important that people have effective ways of dealing with different perspectives and personalities in potentially conflicting situations. If you encounter a difficulty with a coworker, first meet with the individual to discuss your concern. During this meeting you need to identify the problem. Use "I" messages to communicate your feelings. At times, the other person may not even be aware that a problem exists. Once the problem has been defined, it is important to determine the cause of the problem and look for possible solutions. The majority of problems can be solved in this manner.

If the problem is unable to be resolved, the next step is to contact your supervising teacher who will advise you of the proper procedure to follow if the problem cannot be resolved.

You should always try to work out the problem to the best of your ability before involving the coordinators or administrators. If you are unable to work out the problem you will then need to determine the proper procedure that you need to use in order to resolve the situation

"People have one thing in common, they are all different."
-Robert Zend

Chapter 6

The Paraprofessional and the General Education Teacher

Previously general education and special education students received their instruction in two separate classrooms with two separate curriculums. The onset of inclusive education has brought about a great deal of change. Teachers who were accustomed to working alone are no longer isolated in their individual classrooms. Often there is a procession of paraprofessionals, special education teachers, and consultants parading through the classroom during the course of the day. Some classroom teachers may feel uncomfortable teaching in front of their colleagues. Often the general education teachers feel as though they are under constant supervision. These frequent interruptions can be very distracting during group instruction for both the students and the teacher.

Included in this chapter, is some basic information related to working in the classroom environment. The first section discusses working in the classroom environment, the second working with students, and the last section various types of instruction which occur in classroom settings.

Working in the Classroom Environment

Rules

You will need to have the list of rules and student expectations for each classroom. Some of the areas that need to be discussed with the supervising teacher include classroom discipline, turning in assignments, pencil sharpening, bathroom privileges, and behavior management to name only a few. Some teachers are easygoing and have few rules, whereas others may be firm and adhere to specific rules allowing no exceptions.

Consistency is important, especially for the student who receives support from several different adults throughout the school day. Appendix A Form #10, entitled Classroom Information, includes a place to list the class rules along with additional information you will need to work effectively in the classroom. One form should be completed for each classroom. If the teacher simply provides a list, read the list carefully; if you have questions or are unsure about a rule, it is important to clarify it.

Periodically, there may be a student who is unable to follow the classroom rules. This student may have an alternate discipline plan. This plan is developed jointly by the general and special education teachers and may replace the classroom behavior management system. Form #8, entitled Back-Up Discipline Plan which was discussed in the previous chapter, may be implemented in this situation. Copies of this plan should also be distributed to all teachers and paraprofessionals involved with the student.

Establishing a Work Area

The classroom is arranged to promote efficient learning. This arrangement must be flexible enough to accommodate the wide variety of activities which occur daily in the classroom. There will be times when the teacher is providing instruction to a large group of students and you may be involved in reteaching or reviewing material with a small group of students in a separate area. From time to time, you may be asked to create student material, correct student work, or document information for the special education teacher. Given this wide variety of duties, you will need a space in each classroom. Your personal space may consist of a desk, table, or, perhaps, a student desk.

A box of personal supplies will help you to do your job more efficiently. This personal supply box may include pencils, pens, markers, note cards, highlighters, calculator, paper clips, tape, and stapler. Supplies may be added as needed. Folders will be needed to keep general classroom information such as the rules, emergency information, and specific information for individual students. It is important you have this information close at hand, especially during the first few weeks, as you will refer to it frequently.

Special projects may also be left in this area. Often projects may be completed during instruction time, movies, or when you are in the classroom but direct support is not required.

For the majority of paraprofessionals, the work day will coincide with the student's school day. This makes communication difficult, but not impossible. A great deal communication will be in writing. Therefore, you will also need a notebook where notes, comments, changes in lessons plans, and schedules may be written.

Entering and Exiting the Classroom

As the school year begins, most teachers will explain to the students that there will be other adults in the classroom at various times throughout the day. Although some paraprofessionals will be assigned to one classroom, the majority will work with various students in several different classrooms. If you work in various classrooms, you may enter the classroom while a lesson is in progress. It is very important to enter and exit the classroom quietly. Until students are familiar with your presence, their attention may be directed to you. Do not respond to the students as it distracts from the current lesson. At an appropriate time, explain to the individual student(s) the importance of focusing on the lesson, even when adults are entering and leaving the room. If a general education teacher has several students with special needs in the classroom it is important to remember that you are only one of the many adults who provide additional support daily.

The following are common situations you may encounter when entering the class.

Lecture: If the general education teacher is in the middle of a lecture or demonstration, go directly to your workstation and read through the lesson plans or notes for the day. If the student is not required to attend to the lecture, you may have specific instructions on your desk as to what should be done during this time period.

Cooperative groups: If students are working in cooperative groups, determine whether or not your support is needed. If so, help the students before checking messages or talking with the classroom teacher. The majority of students will be able to fully participate in cooperative groups as their roles are predetermined.

Independent or Seatwork Activities: If students are working at their desks, check to see if the students are able to complete the work independently. If not, provide the necessary support. There will be times when the seatwork is not appropriate for the student. Instead of wasting time completing an unsuitable assignment, reteaching may be a better use of the time. The supervising teacher will provide specific materials to complete with individual students.

If the general education teacher is available during independent activities and the students do not need your support, it may be an appropriate time to discuss lessons, assignments, or questions related to specific students. Always remember the rules of confidentiality when discussing issues related to students in the classroom environment.

Working with Students

Student Expectations

It is important to remember that all students can learn. Students should always be challenged and encouraged to do their best work and behave appropriately in the various school settings.

The expectations for students are likely to vary depending upon the setting, activity, and expectations of the immediate supervising teacher. For example, the expectation for a student in a group setting, independent activity, one-on-one activity, and lunchroom may all be different but should remain consistent within the specific activity. It is important to note that the paraprofessional is often the person responsible for upholding expectations. Therefore, it is important to be especially careful not to be lenient on days when you feel particularly calm, happy, or tired. For example, when you are feeling rested, you may overlook a behavior that you may not tolerate when you are tired. When tired, you may allow a student to set an assignment aside because you do not have the patience to deal with the activity; however, when feeling rested you may insist that the student complete the assignment. Students need to know what to expect, and when working with students, consistency is important.

Some conscientious adults feel that when a student is unable to finish an assignment it will reflect personally on their individual skill, and perhaps, affect the evaluation of their job performance. This is not the case. Not all students in the inclusive classroom are able to complete the assigned work. Because of this, the individual work is modified to meet the student's needs. The modified material should be at a level that will be commensurate with the student's ability. If the student is still unable to complete the assignment after it has been modified, it must be analyzed further and additional changes will need to be made. Therefore, it is important that the student is held accountable for work completion and takes the responsibility for turning it in.

At times, a student may not want your assistance, but it is apparent that support is needed. If a student refuses support and it is clear that the student is unable to complete the assignment, there are several options available. You may want to discuss the following options with the supervising teacher in advance.

Option One: Permit the student to complete the entire assignment alone. Check the final quality of the assignment. If the quality is acceptable the student turns in the assignment and the student can be congratulated for completing the work independently. If the student has guessed, filled in answers that have no meaning, or obviously not understood the assignment, it must be redone with assistance. You will encounter times when a student will refuse to redo the assignment. In this case, follow the classroom plan for incomplete assignments. You cannot force a student to complete the assignment, and the student cannot be allowed to only complete the assignments of preference. Do not get into a power struggle with the student. If a student frequently refuses to complete assignments, you will need to set a meeting with the supervising teacher to discuss the situation.

Option Two: Provide support to a small group of students instead of working with the student individually. Thus, the student with special needs is not always singled out.

The special education paraprofessional may provide consistent support only to students who have an Individual Education Plan in place. General education students may periodically be included in the small group settings, but the students must be rotated so they do not become an integral part of the group. If a general education student consistently needs additional support, the general education teacher may choose to use the instructional modifications created for the students in special education for these struggling students also.

Option Three: On occasion, it may be appropriate to change positions with the classroom teacher. From time to time it may be advantageous for the general education teacher to work with a small group of special education students while you monitor the class during independent seatwork activities.

Special education students must be held accountable in the classroom environment. Students should be expected to complete and turn in their assignments and also to act in an appropriate manner.

Establishing a Relationship

Establishing a relationship with the student is important. The greater the trust, the easier it will be to work with the student. It is important to be friendly with students, but not so friendly that the student thinks of you as a peer instead of an adult in an authority position. The boundaries need to be established at the beginning of the relationship, as you will encounter times when you need to be firm and discipline the student. This issue of boundaries is particularly important at the secondary level when the age difference may conceivably be only two to three years.

When working with students in the classroom environment, it is important to be accessible to students but not hover over them. At the elementary level, students frequently derive pleasure from individual assistance. As students grow and mature, some become very conscientious and do not want to appear different. Though the student may still desire special assistance, fitting in with his peers becomes more important. Your major responsibility is to assist the student with special needs, but it is also important to respect and foster independence. Therefore, if the students you support do not need assistance, walk around the classroom and help other students. You may provide support to others, but always remember that your primary area of focus is the student in special education.

Communicating with Students

It is important to establish a positive relationship with students. Your job is to encourage students to do their best. A language of acceptance will help students feel comfortable and at ease. When working with students individually or in small groups, good eye contact is important, as it indicates that you are interested in what the student has to say.

When speaking to a student in the classroom, address the student by name. Do not use terms such as "honey," "dear," or "sport" when talking to students. Speak to students with special needs as you do to students without special needs. Do not talk down to the student, change your tone of voice, or use phrases that are not age appropriate. Students in the general education class are modeling your behavior and are learning from you. If you hear students in the classroom talking down to any student, gently correct them in private. If the problem persists, an inservice may be required for the entire class by the special education department.

There will be times when, communicating with some students, you may need to shorten the length of the sentence, provide directions one step at a time, or leave out confusing details. This is especially true for students with receptive language difficulties or hearing impairments and can easily be implemented without changing your tone of voice.

Types of Classroom Instruction

The majority of classroom instruction takes place in a large group, small group, or in a one-on-one situation.

During large group instruction such as a class lecture, your duties may include notetaking, helping students to stay on task, or monitoring specific students. If a lecture is inappropriate for some students you may be asked to work with individual students during this time period.

As a paraprofessional, the majority of instructional support you provide will be to individual students or small groups of students. There may be times when the classroom teacher is instructing a small group of students and you are asked to monitor a class activity or to provide support to the general population of students. This is perfectly acceptable as long as the supervising teacher is available and physically present in the classroom.

Since the majority of your responsibilities will be with students in small groups, the remainder of this chapter will focus on types of small group instruction that you will encounter in the classroom environment.

Small Group Instruction

One of the primary challenges is to find ways to make instructional activities effective and efficient. Small group instruction increases the amount of instructional time for individual students and allows for increased interaction. Students benefit from small group instruction, as it is a less threatening environment to ask questions, there is more opportunity to respond individually, and the student receives immediate feedback from the adult. With two adults often in the classroom, small groups allow multiple activities to occur simultaneously in the classroom. During small group instruction, the paraprofessional may contribute by working with a small group or by monitoring the students in the classroom while the supervising teacher works with a small group of students.

Small groups are established for a multitude of reasons, and understanding the purpose of the group is vital before your role can be determined. Small groups (two to six students) are highly effective but need to be properly organized and managed. In order for the group to function, the group activity should be properly explained and the students must possess the skills necessary to work effectively in groups. The major advantage of a small group is that it allows the student to participate more frequently and receive an immediate response. Small groups are effective for drill and practice activities, as student responses are easily monitored. Problem-solving activities and brainstorming are effective strategies when working with three or more students, as the students need to listen and respond to the ideas of others.

The duration of a small group varies depending upon the lesson or the assignment. Some small groups are developed to work on one specific lesson or activity. These groups may last one subject block. Once the activity is complete, the composition of the group may change. Other groups will exist for longer periods of time. These groups may include students working on a long-term group project or a group of students involved in a research activity. Decisions about when to change the dynamics of the group will be made by the supervising teacher.

For students to work effectively in a group, there are several basic skills which need to be acquired. Students must be able to take turns and cooperate, follow directions, support one another, and record group performance. Often, these skills need to be taught to students and monitored closely until acquired. The supervising teacher will be able to provide guidelines and suggestions for teaching these skills.

Student groups fluctuate in the classroom environment depending upon the predetermined objective or final outcome desired by the supervising teacher. Often, students in the classroom are grouped in one of the following ways:

Ability Levels: Students are assigned to groups according to their individual ability levels. For example students may be grouped by their reading levels: above-average readers, average readers, and students who need support with reading.

Curriculum Level: Students are assigned to groups related to the type of curriculum or levels so students may work on similar skills in the group.

Individual Differences: Groups are formed to allow selected students to be included with others so they have the opportunity to learn from one's individual differences. This grouping may also be used for students who are continually isolated from their peers.

Random Grouping: Students are assigned randomly to groups. The groups may change so students have experience working with diverse groups of students.

Social Skill Level: Groups are selected so that students may work on social skills in specific situations.

Within the small group settings, several types of instruction may occur. The most common types of small group instruction include cooperative learning groups, mastery learning, multilevel instruction, peer tutoring, real-life learning, and the use of technology. In some of the following narratives, instructional practices, hypothetical goals, and objectives have been included to help clarify the differences between the individual instructional practices. If a student has a separate goal or objective for the small group session, the individual goals and objectives are developed collaboratively between the general and special education teachers. As a paraprofessional will help the student to meet these objectives.

Cooperative Learning Groups

Cooperative learning is a small group instruction technique that allows all students to be included into the classroom with relative ease. With cooperative learning groups the emphasis is placed on the process of learning. The final grade is based on individual effort, group effort, and the final outcome. The number of students included in each cooperative group varies depending upon the unit.

Let's make use of the following example of cooperative learning. Imagine a class is working on measurement during a cooperative science unit. Each group consists of four students. The students are required to measure various liquids and objects.

In this example, the four major responsibilities have been determined in advance by the supervising teacher. The individual responsibilities include gathering materials, collecting data, reading aloud, and recording the information. Please note how easily the student is able to be included (despite the student's limitations) and how students can be actively involved in this type of small group.

Gatherer: One member of the group is assigned to gather materials and set up the activity. The student who has difficulty cooperating in a group situation may be assigned to this specific task; therefore, limits are naturally defined.

Data Collector: One member of the group is assigned to record the specific results from the results achieved. This information is later recorded on the group response sheet. For a student who has difficulty staying on task, this activity may allow movement and keep the student actively involved in the activity. The non-reader may also collect and record the data.

Reader: One member of the group is assigned to read the material aloud. A student who receives support for written language may be assigned to this role. For the student who has difficulty reading the reading no longer interferes. The student is able receive the information auditorily and participate in the lesson.

Recorder: One member of the group is assigned to write the group response. For the student who has difficulty with reading or with written language, the obstacles are removed, as the student is able to contribute his ideas and is a fully active participant.

With cooperative groups, all students are able to participate. The student who functions at a completely different level (such as a student with mental retardation) is still able to participate while working on individual goals or objectives. With the support of the paraprofessional, the student may use this cooperative group to work on goals related to following directions, measuring, counting, and developing language. The student may be able to participate in the following ways:

Following Directions: The student is asked to gather the material needed for the activity. The materials may include items such as measuring cups, rulers, yardsticks, pencils, paper, etc. Depending upon the student's ability, the directions may be one-, two-, or three-step directions.

Measuring: If students are required to measure in centimeters and millimeters, it may be appropriate for a student to measure in inches, feet, or yards. If measuring liquid, the student may be asked to go to the sink and get 1 cup of water which the group may then use to measure smaller quantities such as milliliters.

Counting: If the student is working on counting or number recognition, he may count the number of rulers or yardsticks needed to measure the width of the classroom. If the student is required to gather or put away the materials, he may be responsible for counting the specific objects and returning the objects to their proper location.

Developing Language: The items used for the cooperative group may be used for vocabulary development. The student may practice using the object names in sentences. Depending upon ability the goal may simply be to learn the names of the student in the group.

Mastery Learning

Mastery learning is a teaching strategy used in all classrooms. Mastery learning focuses on a specific skill and allows opportunity for the student to gain mastery at his level through reteaching and reinforcement of the skill. With mastery learning, students are frequently expected to demonstrate their knowledge by completing an exam or some form of assessment (either formal or informal) at the end of the unit.

An example of mastery learning is as follows: *Given 20 sentence, the student will locate the noun and verb in each sentence. The student must score 80% or better to pass the unit.*

With mastery learning, the student with special needs is often able to reach the goal. The difference is that it may be reached in a nontraditional way. For some students instructional modifications will need to be implemented, and for others, the supervising teacher may need to modify the level of mastery. For many students, additional drill and practice exercises may be needed. This additional practice may be completed as a small group activity or individually with the student.

For some students, the level of mastery may be demonstrated by the following methods instead of a traditional paper/pencil exam. Note that in the previous example, the student only needs to demonstrate their knowledge of nouns and verbs. Although the exam conceivably requires reading and writing, the skill actually tested is whether or not the student is able to locate the nouns and verbs in a sentence.

If a student has mastered the skill but is unable to read the material, the student may be partnered with a fluent reader. The test may be read aloud. Another alternative for students who have difficulty reading the test is to select a 20-sentence passage from the student's alternate text and ask the student to identify the nouns and verbs from the passage.

If a student has difficulty writing, test the student orally. Ask him to select ten nouns in the classroom environment, then to observe the actions of the students in the class and state ten verbs.

Another alternative to writing is to allow the student to circle or underline the correct answer if the test involves a large amount of writing.

For the student with a severe discrepancy, the lesson may focus on vocabulary development using nouns and verbs. Cut out pictures from a magazine of nouns such as boy, dog, girl, or toy. Label the pictures. Add a verb to the picture and work on sentence construction. Examples for the listed nouns may include "the boy eats," "the dog plays," "the girl runs," or "the toy spins."

Multilevel Instruction

Multilevel instruction is also used in a small group setting. In multilevel instruction, the supervising teacher provides the instruction to the class. With the focus placed on the key concepts, students demonstrate their knowledge through presentations, projects, or assigned activities. The outcome for the student with special needs may be simple or complex. This type of instruction is appropriate for special education students.

Let's look at a simple example of multilevel instruction in a teaching unit relating to volcanoes. *The class is required to learn about the formation of volcanoes, locate active and inactive volcanoes, and learn ten vocabulary words associated with the lesson.* This is the final outcome for the general population of students in the classroom.

For some students with special needs, this lesson may or may not be appropriate. Following are examples for two hypothetical students in the same classroom, Jeremy and Sarah. Jeremy is able to meet the goal with minimal modifications. Sarah, on the other hand, is performing at a level 4-5 years below that of her peer group. When a lesson is inappropriate for a student with special needs, a separate goal is developed by the special education team for the student. Form #11 in Appendix A is a worksheet where the goals and objectives may be listed.

The goal for Jeremy, developed by the supervising teacher in this hypothetical situation might be: *Jeremy will demonstrate how a volcano is formed, locate active and inactive volcanoes, and learn a minimum of five new vocabulary words from the class list.* The goal for Jeremy is the same as for the general education students with the exception of the number of vocabulary words, which has been modified by the special education teacher. Even though the final outcome is almost identical, the way the Jeremy arrives at the final outcome may be different.

Once the goal is determined the objectives are written. The objectives are the steps the student will take to meet the final goal. Take a look at the goal and objectives written for Jeremy.

Goal: Jeremy will demonstrate how a volcano is formed and learn five or more new vocabulary words from the class list.

> **Objective 1:** The student is required to listen to the class lecture and use diagrams from supplemental texts in place of reading the textbook.

> **Objective 2:** The student is required to listen to the textbook chapter on tape or join a small group and listen to the text as it is read aloud.

> **Objective 3:** The student will use a map to locate active and inactive volcano locations.

Objective 4: The student will create a model or diagram of a volcano in place of a paper-and-pencil test. The model will demonstrate the student's knowledge of the five preselected vocabulary words.

As a paraprofessional you may be required to provide support to Jeremy in the classroom. Reread objectives 1-4 and think about ways in which you may be asked to support Jeremy in the classroom. List your responses and then compare your responses to the possible responses listed below.

_____
_____
_____
_____
_____
_____
_____
_____
_____

Some of your possible responsibilities may include but are not limited to the following:

- Record the textbook chapter so that Jeremy is able to listen to the chapter on tape.

- Read the chapter aloud with Jeremy or with a small group of students.

- Find additional resource books in the library related to volcanoes.

- Help to locate the volcanoes on a map.

- Practice using the vocabulary words in sentences.

- Provide additional drill and practice activities.

In the next example Sarah is unable to complete the assignment. Sarah has mental retardation; therefore, both her developmental and cognitive abilities severely lag behind those of her peer group. Sarah is still able to participate in the unit even though her goal and objectives are different. Sara's goals and objectives may be related to vocabulary development, fine motor development, visual discrimination, and social skills. The following example includes a goal and several objectives which may be appropriate for a student who performs significantly below grade level.

Goal: Sarah will be able to distinguish between a mountain, a desert, and a prairie.

Objective 1: The student will look at various pictures of mountains, deserts, and prairies. The student will be able to point to pictures of mountains. (Vocabulary development and visual discrimination)

Objective 2: The student will create a book with pictures of mountains, deserts, and prairie. The student will dictate a sentence describing each geographical area. (Fine motor skills and language development)

Some examples of descriptions may include:

- A mountain is very big. Sometimes there is snow on the top. Some people go to mountains to ski.

- The desert is very hot and dry. There is no grass. Cactus grows in the desert. A desert has very little rain.

- The prairies are flat. Grass and flowers grow on the prairies.

Objective 3: The student will formulate sentences alone or with assistance. The student may copy sentences from examples or trace over previously written sentences. (Written language and fine motor)

Objective 4: The student will be able to distinguish between a picture of a mountain and an active volcano. (Visual Discrimination)

Objective 5: The student will create a model mountain out of modeling clay and share her model with the class. (Social Skills)

Sarah is participating in the classroom even though the goal and objectives are different than her peers.

As a paraprofessional you will be required to provide support to Sarah in the classroom. Reread the objectives and think about ways in which you may be asked to support Sarah's meeting the goal listed. List your responses and then compare your responses to the possible responses listed below.

_____
_____
_____
_____
_____
_____
_____
_____
_____
_____

Some of your possible responsibilities may include, but are not limited to, the following:

- Help find pictures in magazines.

- Assist with cutting, pasting, and creating a geography book.

- Find pictures, when possible, of the vocabulary words.

- Practice using the vocabulary words in sentences.

- Monitor seatwork activities.

- Write the sentences dictated by the student.

- Practice several sentences verbally for the student to use in the final class presentation.

Peer Tutoring and Leadership Opportunities

Peer tutoring is used in many classroom settings. Often students learn by teaching others. This can be a positive experience for both the tutor and the person receiving the tutoring. Peer tutors can lend support to students with special needs. Training must be provided for the tutors so they learn how to guide the student but do not complete the work for them.

Students with special needs should have the experience of being tutor and a leader. This opportunity may occur in or outside of the student's classroom. As you discover the strengths and special talents of each student, share this information with the classroom teacher. The classroom teacher will be able to place the student in a tutorial or leadership role.

- Provide opportunities for the student to read to or tutor younger students. Assist the student with the selection of appropriate materials.
  For example, if a student has mastered basic sight words, the student could help in a primary classroom by providing drill and practice support.

- The student with artistic ability may demonstrate specific techniques or teach an art activity to a small group of students.

- The student who excels in math may tutor those who have difficulty.

- The student with natural athletic ability may demonstrate techniques or skill areas to the rest of the class.

- A student who uses specialized materials such as communication tools, Braille, or a wheelchair can demonstrate their uses to the class. If possible, obtain a second wheelchair and allow students to use it. Provide supplemental books in Braille. Ask the student to read the books to the class. Allow classmates the opportunity to also learn Braille. A student with a communication board can demonstrate the how the board functions. Following the demonstration, allow the student to teach others how to use it. If a student uses sign language, have the student teach the class a sign a day and incorporate the signing techniques into the classroom.

Students should also have the opportunity to be placed into leadership roles. Once again, the activity may take place in or outside of the classroom.

- For the student who is unable to read fluently, a primary level book may be selected for the student. The student can practice reading the book aloud and then read it to students in the primary grades. For students who may have a developmental delay, the student may turn the pages for a peer while the peer reads aloud.

- A student with strong verbal skills may lead a discussion group.

- If a student excels in music or the arts, provide an opportunity for a lead in a class play or to play a solo.

- A student who has athletic ability may be a captain of a team or lead a practice session for students who would like to increase their ability.

All students should have the opportunity to teach others. Many times students with disabilities are always on the receiving end. All students have their strengths. It is important to capitalize on these strengths and provide every student the opportunity to be a leader.

Real-Life Learning

Real-life learning may also commonly be referred to as activity-based learning. With this method, the student practices and learns the skill in actual or simulated settings. Examples of activity-based learning may include:

- Teaching measurement through cooking

- Teaching the concept of money by creating a class store

- Providing actual job training on the site

Skill Reinforcement

Reinforcement of previously learned skills commonly occurs in small group settings. Reinforcement of a lesson may include preteaching material to the student, providing additional drill and practice, reteaching, and reviewing materials. Small groups may also be used to support students with incomplete assignments. In a small group, it is simple to confirm individual understanding of the concept. Often, students who constantly are behind with assignments may be able to complete several assignments orally (which perhaps the mainstream class was required to complete in writing) in a minimal period of time. If the assignment is to ascertain whether the student knows the material, knowledge can successfully be checked orally.

Technology

Technology is often used for curriculum support. Computers are a terrific tool for students, as the programs provide immediate feedback which is important for many students. Whether using the computer individually or as a class, programs can be provided for all students at their current levels of performance. Many programs used for drill and practice activities will not allow the student to proceed until a specific criterion has been met. Computers are also appropriate for students who experience difficulty with spelling or fine motor skills as the student is able produce a quality assignment without worrying about penmanship or numerous misspelled words.

Notes

"If there is anything a man can do well, I say let him do. Give him a chance."
- Abraham Lincoln

Chapter 7

Modifications

In the previous six chapters, the word modification has been used freely, and little distinction was made between the various types of modifications. It has been noted that students identified with special needs often require modifications to the curriculum, the instructional techniques, or the environment in order to be successful in the classroom. At this time, you may wonder what exactly a modification is and why do we modify for some students and not others? A modification is simply defined as any change made to the curriculum, instruction, or environment. Students with special needs often learn differently and may need additional support in order to be successful in the classroom. Special education students are not the only students who receive additional support in the classroom environment. Some students may receive assistance from programs such as Title I, or English-as-a-Second Language (ESL), or perhaps have a special 504 Plan. These students require many of the same types of instructional modifications, but their service is provided by the supervising teacher or a paraprofessional who may work in another department.

Instructional and Curricular Modifications

There are several types of modifications for students. The first is a continuous or permanent accommodation. Some examples of continuous accommodations may include the use of a communication device to speak, a computer to write, or a wheelchair for mobility. These accommodations are permanent and used both in and out of school.

Modifications which occur in the classroom may also be subdivided into two additional categories, instructional modifications and curricular modifications.

Instructional modifications are intended to assist students with their daily work. Instructional modifications may include adapting the material so that the student is better able to understand and/or complete the assignment. They may also include reading a test to a student or providing additional support for a specific project or in a specific subject area. These short and preplanned modifications will frequently be carried out by the paraprofessional in the classroom environment. There will be times when a student needs an instructional modification to complete an assignment and other times when the student is able to complete the assignment alone. Therefore, instructional modifications are continually adjusted to meet the needs of the student. Providing instructional modifications will be a daily part of your job.

Curricular modifications are different from instructional modifications as they include concrete changes to the actual curriculum and are determined in advance by the special education team. When a curricular modification is developed the student may have an assignment that is totally different than that of his peers. With curricular modifications the final outcome for the individual student may be the same as for the peers or it may be totally different from the final goal of the others in the classroom environment.

Since not all situations can be anticipated, there may also be on-the-spot instructional modifications in response to an activity that is about to occur or occurring at the moment. Let's take a look at two hypothetical situations.

Melissa is frustrated and struggling with the reading level in the science textbook. Your instructions are to allow Melissa to read the material independently and then help her answer the questions at the end of the chapter. You note that she is becoming increasingly frustrated, so you quietly approach her and ask if she would like your help reading the unfamiliar words. While helping her, you notice that when the material is read aloud, she grasps the main idea quickly. Therefore, it seems the main interference is the textbook reading level and not the actual content of the material. You decide to read the chapter aloud even though it is not one of the instructional modifications listed for Melissa. With the additional reading support, she is able to complete the assignment and answer the discussion questions.

The preceding example would be considered an on-the-spot modification for the student. As a paraprofessional, you had to determine whether to help the student with the assignment or allow the student to struggle and help with only the chapter questions. In this short example, it is difficult to determine if the student needed only a little additional support with the reading level or whether the curriculum is becoming too difficult. Thus, it is important to document this information and to share it with the supervising teacher. When documenting, you will need to ascertain (to the best of your ability) why the student was experiencing difficulty with the reading (reading level was too high, student was unable to sound out unknown words), the type of mistakes the student was encountering (was unable to sound out new vocabulary introduced in bold-faced print), and the results that occurred when the material was read aloud (student was able to easily answer questions at the end of the chapter when the material was read aloud). The following sample of Form #12 – Instructional Changes (located in Appendix A) may be used to report the information. This information will help the supervising teacher plan and adapt the lesson more efficiently and will also document and help to determine whether future curriculum needs to be modified to meet the individual student's needs.

Form #12 Sample

Date: _____

Student: _____

Subject Area: _____

Area of Difficulty Be Specific	Instructional Modification Implemented	Result
Science textbook. Reading level was too difficult. Student was unable to sound out unfamiliar words from the text book and was struggling with the reading level.	First I helped the student figure out the unfamiliar words. Since the student was frustrated and behind in her work, I read the second part of the textbook aloud to her.	Student was able to answer the questions at the end of the chapter without searching for the answers.

You may also encounter times, when working with students, it is necessary to deviate from the planned lesson instead of making an on-the-spot modification. The termination of an assignment may occur because a student has not acquired the basic skills to complete the assignment, the student completes part of the assignment and it is completely wrong, the student is too distressed to complete the assignment, or the student refuses to do the activity. Since it is the responsibility of the supervising teacher(s) to develop the lesson and provide the materials, it is not appropriate for the paraprofessional to create new activities or redesign individual lessons. If a student does not have the basic skills to complete an assignment, the supervising teacher will need to be contacted before continuing with the lesson. You may encounter times that the classroom supervising teacher prefers not to make a decision regarding the curriculum and would like the response to come from the special education team. Since the special education teacher may not be available on short notice, what should be done? It is important to have an alternate plan in place so valuable learning time is not lost. To prepare for this situation alternative work folders are often created. The folders may include previous incomplete assignments, drill and practice activities for previously learned skills, educational games or activities, review activities, or homework. The material in the work folder can also be used when a student completes an assignment before the allotted lesson time is over. It is important to note here that some students are very adept in finding ways to delay a lesson with the intention of avoiding it altogether. Therefore, when terminating a lesson, the paraprofessional should document the reason, and the supervising teacher should be contacted so adjustments can be made prior to subsequent lessons.

Now let's look at another example which requires deviation from the original lesson plan.

> **Example:** The students are preparing for a social studies group project. Each student has been assigned a specific job in the cooperative group. As the students gather the materials, the fire alarm sounds, which of course disrupts the preplanned social studies activity. When the students return to the classroom, there is not enough time to complete the social studies project, so the teacher decides to use the remaining class period for silent reading. Scott (a student you support) does not have a book for independent reading. Since you do not want to lose valuable learning time, a suitable activity must be determined. Several options come to mind. In your personal work folder, you notice that there are vocabulary flashcards intended to reinforce the vocabulary after the social studies activity. After a quick glance, you decide that the cards could be used to preview the vocabulary instead. You note that Scott has a book for silent reading time, but the book is too difficult for him to read alone, so you could also offer to read the book aloud. Scott also has a work folder with make-up work and several assignments which need corrections. Since all three activities seem appropriate, you decide to ask Scott which activity he would prefer to do for the remaining 20 minutes of class.

This situation requires an on-the-spot change in which you need to deviate from the normal class activity. The vocabulary cards, although developed for review, could easily be used for preview. Making corrections to the assignments in the work folder is an appropriate choice. Since the students are reading silently, it would also be appropriate to find a quiet area and read his book aloud. In this example, the paraprofessional can easily make a decision and select an appropriate activity. The only follow-up needed is to contact the supervising teacher and determine an appropriate book so the student has one available for the next silent reading block.

Categories of Modifications

The modifications which occur in the classroom can be grouped into categories. Keep in mind when reading about the following types of modifications that there will be overlap. The areas of modification from the most common to the most complex, include reinforcing the content area, adapting the content area, developing an alternative curriculum, and developing parallel activities. The development of parallel activities is often for students who may participate in the classroom environment but whose final goal is different from the goal of their peers.

Reinforcing the Content Area: Modifications in this area are usually instructional modifications. Often, reinforcing the general education curriculum allows the student to complete the required assignments either alone, with support, or with some instructional modifications. As a paraprofessional, you will be responsible for carrying out many of these modifications daily.

The most common instructional modification is reinforcement of the content area. Frequently this reinforcement will be implemented with individual students or in a small group setting. Often, a small amount of additional reinforcement is all the support a student may need to complete assignments and fulfill the class requirements. Reinforcing the content area also includes previewing, preteaching, and reteaching. Supplemental aids such as study guides, outlines, or audiocassettes are may also be used as reinforcement tools.

Previewing material means that you will look through the material with the student before it is presented in the classroom. The bold-faced vocabulary words and their meanings may be discussed. Captions are read aloud and the bold subject headings discussed. If there are questions at the end of the story or unit, attention may be directed to these so the student knows what he will be held responsible to learn. In the previewing stage, it is helpful to ask the student to recall as much information as possible about the specific topic, so the new concepts can be associated with previously learned knowledge.

Preteaching material helps the student to understand the concept before it is actually taught. For example, if the upcoming lesson is related to prepositions, you may provide the student with simple examples of prepositions and ask the student to use them in sentences. In social studies, science, or reading, the vocabulary could be discussed and pretaught so the student has the necessary background information for the upcoming unit. When preteaching vocabulary, it should always be taught in the context of the textbook, especially if words have multiple meanings.

Reteaching material takes place after the lesson has been presented. At times, classroom instruction and guided practice sessions do not provide sufficient practice for the student with special needs. As you work through assignments individually, you will be able to determine if the student missed a step in a process and, perhaps, to identify the specific type of error that is causing difficulty.

Adapting the Content Area: It is the responsibility of the special education team to determine whether or when curriculum modifications are implemented. Modifying or changing the actual curriculum is not the responsibility of the paraprofessional. Therefore, in this category the actual changes to the curriculum will be made by the team. You, in turn, may be responsible for implementing the instructional modifications to the adapted material.

When adapting the content area, the team may decide that some assignments should be shortened, others may be completed in a small group with assistance, and, in some cases that the student is not required to complete the assignment at all. In the area of spelling, the student may be required to learn a modified list of words and may spend the week completing drill and practice activities in place of the required classroom activities. The student may dictate answers to a modified list of questions and someone may write them for the student. Certain assignments may be completed orally to check for comprehension instead of having to give the answers in a written format.

Alternative Curriculum: In this category, supplemental materials and activities may be provided to the student. The supplemental materials may have similar content to the general education curriculum but contain a limited vocabulary or have a lower readability level. The materials will be provided by the supervising teacher.

Parallel Curriculum: For some students the final outcome of the lesson or activity may be completely different, even though the student may perform the same type of activity as his peers. For example, a student with a parallel curriculum may be required to listen to a story on tape while the students in the class are required to read the material alone. When unaware of the student's IEP goal, it may appear that the student is not actively involved in the classroom activity. Upon reviewing the student's IEP, the goal for this student may be to listen quietly for a predetermined amount of time and raise his hand when called upon. In reality, the final goal for the student may be a socialization goal instead of an academic goal. A student with a fine motor goal may work on letter formation, use templates, or create objects with clay, while his peers are writing a story. The student with a parallel math curriculum may use the calculator to perform basic math operations, while class is performing advanced math calculations. In this case, the student's goal may be to learn and use the functions of the calculator. Often, students with a parallel curriculum have functional goals on their IEPs. Functional goals are often based on the skills a student will need to live independently as an adult in a supervised apartment or a group home.

In summary, there are two main types of modifications which occur in the classroom environment, and these modifications apply to a variety of situations and subject areas. The instructional modifications provided in the classroom environment will help the student to complete the various classroom assignments. Often the student completes the same assignment as his peer group, but with additional support. These modifications frequently appear in many areas. For example, if a student requires material to be taped or read aloud in Social Studies, this will probably apply to other subject areas as well. The student who needs help organizing thoughts on paper will probably need help with stories, research papers, and, perhaps, o essay exams. The second type of modification is a curricular modification. With curricular modifications, the direct changes are actually made to the student's curriculum. These modifications are more obvious; the assignment frequently appears different when compared to the assignment for the general education students. The special education team is responsible for making curricular modifications and will provide the material. You will be responsible for providing support to the student in the classroom.

A modification which helps one student may not apply to the next student, as modifications are created and developed for individual students and are based on each student's Individual Education Plan. In the classroom, students who do not receive service under the umbrella of special education may also receive modifications to the curriculum, but these modifications are provided under the direction of the general education teacher or another specialist such as the ESL or Title I teacher. The special education students are your primary responsibility. Periodically, additional students join the group for drill and practice activities, specific skill work, preteaching, and review activities.

Frequently Asked Questions

Often, questions arise related to instructional modifications. Frequently, the questions are specific; therefore, it is difficult to provide an answer, as the response will vary depending upon the student, the classroom, and the supervising teacher. Some of the most frequently asked questions related to making instructional modifications are listed here.

Is it okay to work with students who are not special education students?

At times you may be reviewing a lesson, providing drill and practice activities, or reinforcing a specific skill that would benefit general education students as well. Therefore, you may be asked to include additional students in your group. This is perfectly acceptable as long as the students do not become a permanent part of the special education group. When working with general education students, the guidelines for the students are provided by the general education teacher and not the special education teacher.

How do I know if I have modified the activity too much or too little?

At times, you may question how much or how little instructional support to provide for a student. For example, you may wonder if an entire passage should be read aloud or whether to help the student only with the difficult words. When uncertain, use your best judgment, and then increase or decrease the amount of support. The longer you work with the student the more skilled you will become.

What do I do if the student is unable to complete the assignment even with prompts and support?

It is appropriate for the paraprofessional to guide the student and provide support but the assignment should never be completed for the student. If the student is unable to complete the work, it may be an indicator that the work is still too difficult and needs to be modified by the supervising teacher. If the student is unable to complete the assignment, put it aside and talk to the supervising teacher before the next class session.

The student seems to be able to do the work independently, so what should I do during the class period?

If the student is able to complete the work without support, step back and allow the student to do so. Spot check the student's work periodically for accuracy. It is important for students to recognize that support is available when needed, but it is also very important to encourage and foster independence. Therefore, do not hover over the student if he is able to do the work independently. Instead, use the time to walk around the class and help others who may need some assistance.

I don't feel comfortable in some classrooms because I don't know the subject material. What should I do?

Often, you will work across grade levels and curriculum areas. Therefore you are not expected to be an expert in every field. There may be times when you will want to read through specific chapters and access the Teacher's Guide so that you can preview the unit before it is taught.

When working with students in an area such as mathematics, you may want to review skills before trying to help the student. Often you will be in the classroom for the instruction component, so you will be able to learn right along with the students.

The next chapter includes multiple ideas which will help you when working in the classroom environment.

"Every job is a self-portrait of the person who did it. Autograph your work with excellence." – unknown

Chapter 8

Getting Organized

Before working with students, some basic information about the individual student need to be compiled, and it is essential to know the type of support to help the student expectations. Typically, each paraprofessional is responsible for supporting a number of students in various classrooms throughout the day. Therefore, it is important to document the instructional modifications for each student in order to avoid confusion.

Once your role has been determined, you will be ready to work with the student. During the course of the year, materials will be created as well as received from the supervising teachers. Therefore, it is also important to determine how the material can be organized and saved for future reference.

Organization of the Modifications

In Appendix A, Forms #13-16 may be used to document the modifications listed in the student's IEP. The ready-to-use forms include both a narrative and a checklist version. The forms also may be used as a guideline if you would like to develop your own. The information documented on the forms must be provided to you by the supervising teacher, as the information is derived from the student's IEP. Once the information is complete, the supervising teacher will determine whether the forms should be photocopied and distributed to all team members. In some situations, the supervising teacher may only provide a list of instructional modifications. If you are provided with a list, be sure to clarify the procedures and expectations before meeting with the student. The form in Appendix A may be used to compile the information. If a form is being used and it contains personal reminders and notes, do not make copies to distribute unless you have permission from a certified team member.

Since all students are unique, separate forms need to be filled out for each individual student. The forms will be referred to frequently (especially during the first couple of weeks), so keep them close at hand during the work day. The information is confidential so it must be stored in a secure place. The forms will need to be updated periodically.

Organization of Material

During the course of the school year, supplemental materials will be developed for students. If the materials has not been cataloged and previously saved, it is important to create a filing system for the future. Materials such as vocabulary and spelling flashcards are easy to make and store, and will be used until a new curriculum is adopted by the school district. Some materials are more time-consuming to create. For example, a student may need a special audiocassette such as a paraphrased version which highlights only the most important information in the textbook or possibly an audiocassette that corresponds to a specific study guide. These will need to be created. Customized audiocassettes may take an hour or more to create. Often, the classroom textbooks and novels are available for purchase directly from the publisher if the budget allows. Cataloging and saving the material takes additional time but will save time in the future, as the material is available for all students and teachers. This section includes some ways to save and store the material for future reference.

Material is easily organized into 4" three-ring notebooks. Label each notebook by subject and classroom teacher. Insert pocket folders or clear transparency holders into the three-ring notebook. Label and insert tabs to identify each unit. As modified or supplemental materials are created, insert the material into the corresponding pocket. Each year, material can be added to the notebook.

Index cards can easily be stored in small recipe boxes. Label each recipe box with the subject area such as *Grade 3 Spelling Words, Grade 8 Social Studies Vocabulary with Definitions* or *Dolch Sight Words.*

What should be saved? The answer is simple. Save everything that may be used for review or with additional students in the future. Materials may include:

- index cards with vocabulary words on the front and definitions on the back, spelling and sight word drill and practice cards, and bold-faced words from the student textbooks

- individual audiocassettes of textbooks or novels

- discussion questions (with answers) for individual units with page numbers and location clues

- modified study guides, teacher-created units, and corresponding assessment material

- lists of supplemental materials used to reinforce and supplement the unit

- worksheets and supplemental material used for reinforcement

- games and related activities created to reinforce skills

Often, school district personnel will make additional copies of the adapted material to store in a central location so all educators may access the material. The central storage location is often located in the district special education office. When copies of audiocassettes, modified assessments, and units are stored in a central location, individual teachers may make copies or check out audiocassettes, if needed.

Notes

"There is a brilliant child locked inside every student."
-Marva Collins

Chapter 9

Helping All Students Learn

As you learned in Chapter 7, there are several categories of modifications which range from simple to complex. The remainder of this publication includes many ideas to implement in the classroom environment. Since all students are unique, a successful strategy for one student may not be applicable for another. Therefore, the intent of the remainder of this book is to provide a potpourri of ideas from which to choose. The ideas are grouped by category and numbered for quick and easy reference.

Textbook Modifications

Many students with special needs encounter difficulty in the area of reading. Since reading encompasses a major part of each school day, textbook modifications are critical if the student is to experience success throughout the school day. The following ideas are applicable for most textbooks.

Prereading Stage

You may encounter students with a large discrepancy between their individual ability and that of their peers. If the student is unable to read or write, many of the activities listed in this section are inappropriate. For these students, you may want to read through the section entitled Prewriting Stage which begins with Idea #68. The ideas listed in the prewriting stage section include activities for the introduction of letters and sound/symbol relationships, as well as some basic prereading and prewriting suggestions.

For students who are unable to read an optional prereading program is *Phonemic Awareness: Lessons, Activities and Games* by Victoria Groves Scott. The scripted 20-minute lessons are appropriate for individuals or for small groups of students who are non-readers. Phonemic awareness training may be used as a prerequisite to reading or for elementary students who have not had success with traditional reading programs. There is also an inservice video, *Phonemic Awareness: The Sounds of Reading* which demonstrates how to teach phonemic awareness and apply the principles of the program in the classroom. This resource is listed in Appendix B.

Creating Audiocassettes

Audiocassettes are a valuable tool for students. Students who experience difficulty reading may use the audiocassettes during the school day and take the tapes home to review materials for upcoming tests. Often, audiocassettes can be purchased directly from the textbook publishers. If they are not available, you may be asked to make them. If you are asked to make audiocassettes, it is an advantage, as it provides a way to obtain a comprehensive overview of the curriculum. Audiocassettes are not only valuable to students with special needs, but they also provide support to students who have been absent from class.

The supervising teacher will determine the format that best meets the needs of the individual student. If study guidelines, comprehension checkpoints, vocabulary, and other pertinent information are required for the audiocassette, the supervising teacher will provide this information to you. Before creating audiocassettes, read the following suggestions:

1. Select a high quality audiocassette for the original recording. Label the original and store it in a safe place. Less expensive cassettes may be used for copies as these frequently are misplaced by students.

2. When preparing audiocassettes, read in a clear voice. Find a quiet place with no distractions. Record several minutes of silence and then listen to the recording. Is the recorder picking up background noise? If background noises such as doors closing, telephones ringing, or conversations are apparent, change locations.

3. Textbook material should be read at approximately 120-175 words per minute. Practice by selecting a passage of approximately 150 words. Read the passage several times while using a timer to calculate the reading speed. When you have finished, listen to the recording. Make sure the audiocassette is clear and easily understood. This is not as easy as it seems. A good audiocassette is difficult to create.

4. The audiocassette should begin with a statement of the title, chapters, and page numbers recorded on the tape (i.e., Grade 3 - Social Studies - Chap.1, pgs. 7-18). The audiocassette should also be labeled. The labeling system should be consistent for each cassette to simplify the filing. It is important to have a duplicate copy in case of loss. These tapes will continue to be used in the upcoming years.

5. Often, a list of study guidelines is recorded at the beginning of the audiocassette. This helps orient the student to the main points of the section. The study guideline may include the key vocabulary words listed in bold type and the study questions

located at the end of each unit. If there is a written study guide for the unit, the guide should be filed with the cassette.

6.   Comprehension checkpoints such as *"Please stop the tape here and list three uses of water,"* may be listed on the on the tape If this format is used, a study guide may be provided to the student with the corresponding checkpoints and answers. Another option is to record the checkpoint answers after the pause on the recorded audiocassette. The supervising teacher will provide the objectives of the lesson and will help to determine where the specific checkpoints should be located.

7.   Ask whether an extra textbook is available for special education students. On the inside front cover, place an index card with the key symbols that relate to specific portions of the audiocassette. For example:

- an asterisk (*) may indicate a portion of the text that has been paraphrased on audiocassette

- the pound sign (#) may indicate that the student should stop and give the definition for a word in bold type.

The special education and general education teachers will determine the symbols to be used on the book key.

8.   If a student is required to read the material alone, alternate pages of the textbook may be recorded. This allows the student to listen to one page and read one page either silently or aloud. Be sure to note on the audiocassette label that the recording contains only alternate pages. Alternate page audiocassettes help the student who is able to read but is struggling to keep up with day-to-day reading.

9.   Paraphrase the entire text, with simplified vocabulary for the student who is unable to read. The supervising teacher will provide the main objectives of the lesson. When paraphrasing, include only the most important material. Talk about the pictures, boldfaced print, and diagrams. Paraphrasing is difficult and will need to be practiced before attempting to record the material.

Previewing or Preteaching Materials in Advance

Materials often can be previewed with the student. Previewing helps the student to acquire a basic understanding of the concept before it is presented in the classroom.

10.   Create an audiocassette of the predetermined assignment. Allow the student to take the audiocassette home before the material is read in class. If the student is familiar with the main characters, story, and plot, it will be easier to understand the material when presented by the general education teacher.

11. Preview and discuss pictures in textbooks before material is read in class. Ask the student to tell you as much as possible about the subject. For example, if the story is about crossing the Atlantic Ocean on a ship, ask the student what they know about ships and oceans. How does an ocean look, sound, feel, smell, and taste? Has the student ever been on a ship? If so, what did it feel like; what did they see, hear, taste, or touch? Try to relate new concepts to previous experiences and build on the student's prior knowledge whenever possible.

12. Review the boldfaced words from the reading material. Practice reading the new words. Define and discuss the vocabulary in the context of the unit. Practice using the words in sentences directly related to the textbook material. It is important to have a teacher's guide or student book so words with multiple meanings are defined within the context of the unit. For example, assume that you have a list of vocabulary words without specific definitions. The list includes the following words: bluff, stern, and bear. Which definition would you use?

Word	Definition #1	Definition #2
bluff	steep bank or cliff	fool or mislead
stern	rear part of a ship	harsh; strict
bear	large animal	support; carry

Now assume that the student has told you the topic is early explorers. Look at the words and their definitions in the previous chart. What definition should be taught? Even if the subject is defined, it would be difficult to select the correct meaning without a teacher's guide.

13. Provide a list of discussion questions to the student before the student reads the text. Skim the material and help the student locate the answers by including the page numbers and clues with discussion questions.

14. Ask the general or special education teacher for a student textbook in which to write. Highlight important information in the textbook. Color-code the student textbook. An example follows:

Color Key
(Tape the key into the front of the textbook)
yellow - vocabulary words
blue – definitions
green - topic sentences, important facts, and test information

15. Generate a list of new vocabulary words and provide an outline of the main ideas for each unit. This can be used as a take-home study guide.

16. In some classrooms, students are required to read the material aloud. If reading aloud during class causes anxiety for the student, select several paragraphs from

the unit to practice. Provide the list with the specific paragraphs to the supervising teacher. Later, if the student is required to read aloud, he is prepared.

17. After reading a paragraph or section of a textbook, ask the student to paraphrase the material. Paraphrasing will help the student to recall the material, as the student is restating the main ideas using his own vocabulary. The RAP acronym that follows will help the student to remember the three steps involved.

> **R**ead the paragraph
> **A**sk yourself to recall the main idea and several details about the material
> **P**ractice saying the main ideas and important details in your own words.

18. Ask the supervising teacher for an additional set of textbooks that can either be checked out or remain at home for personal use.

On-the-Spot Textbook Modifications

At times, you may not have an opportunity to preview materials with students in advance. The following strategies will assist the students with the material in the classroom setting during the actual lesson.

19. Read the text aloud using a guided reading procedure. This method is appropriate for a small group of struggling readers. With this method the students are guided step by step through the material. As the material is read aloud, stop frequently to ask questions, summarize and paraphrase the information, and ask questions to check for understanding.

20. At times, the class may be divided into two separate groups. The students with special needs may be divided into or remain in one group. If working in small groups, it is important that the supervising teacher provides a copy of the discussion questions so students are receiving and discussing the same information. This allows for maximum active participation of all students.

21. As students read aloud, allow the student who experiences difficulty with reading to "pass or play" when his turn arrives. The student with special needs may not be comfortable reading in front of a large group. As the comfort level increases, risks will be taken. If the student is required to read aloud, strategically seat the student near someone who is able to help the student decode the unknown words.

22. Provide an outline of the textbook material for the student. Allow the student to take notes on the outline while peers are reading aloud.

23. Supplemental materials may be available in a high-interest, low-vocabulary format. These materials are often listed in the Teacher's Guides under supplementary resources.

24.   Often it is appropriate to record material while it is read and discussed during the actual class period. This is a time saver as the material and the class discussion are recorded for future use. This also supports the student who is absent.

25.   Prepare an outline of important material for the student to use as a guide when listening to materials.

Novels and Free-Choice Reading

Many classrooms have a silent reading time block incorporated into the daily class schedule. At the secondary levels, entire class periods may be devoted to reading material directly related to subject areas. For students with special needs, this time should also be productive, even if the student needs assistance and support is not available for the entire class period. If a student with special needs is unable to read the material alone, often the student will "pretend" to read the material. When this happens, the class period is often wasted, and the student usually ends up completing the assignment at home.

26.   Ask students to record their favorite books and novels. The books may be placed in a classroom library or the media center for students to check out. These taped books are an alternative for students during silent reading time.

        At the secondary level, students may also record required classroom novels for classroom libraries.

27.   If there is a non-reader in the class, read aloud to a small group of students. Vary the students in the group. Allow the student to choose a friend to participate in the group.

28.   Check the school or local library for videotapes of current class novels or stories. A small group of students may view the video instead of reading the material. Students may then compare and contract the storylines of the book and the video.

29.   If assistance is not available, the general education teacher may appoint a student to be the *Teacher for the Day*. This student can read the material aloud to a small group or to an individual student. Use the student checklist, Form #17 in Appendix A, to record the names of volunteers. Allow all students an opportunity to be the *Teacher for the Day*.

Tracking Difficulties

Frequently, students have difficulty following along during read-aloud activities. For some students, the reading level of the classroom textbook is too difficult. For this student it may be easier for the student to listen and obtain the information auditorily. For other students, directionality has not been established. The student may not be sure where to begin reading, try to read from right to left, or have difficulty moving from line to line. The student may continually lose his place. You may feel as though you are continually redirecting the student. If this occurs, the student is probably experiencing difficulty with visual tracking.

30. Partner the student with a peer so they may share the textbooks. The peer can guide the student.

31. Provide oral location clues when reading aloud. Redirect the student by pointing out page and paragraph numbers frequently. For example, "Please begin reading on page 54, paragraph 2."

32. During read-aloud time, frequently check to see if the student is in the correct place. If you are not available, the student should be paired with another student or seated near the general education teacher so tracking can be easily monitored.

33. A bookmark will help the student to keep his place.

34. Draw a horizontal arrow running from the left to the right on an index card. This will help the student with directionality.

35. Cut a window into an index card. The window will help the student to focus on one line of text material at a time. Since all books have different font size the student will need one custom-made card per textbook.

36. Make a "picture frame" cut-out with construction paper. The student will be able to see several lines of print, yet block out the distracting stimuli.

37. Allow the student to listen to the material and view the pictures while someone else reads aloud.

Students with Hearing Impairments
The following suggestions will provide additional support for the student with a hearing impairment.

38. The student should be seated near the teacher.

39. Use visual signals frequently to secure the student's attention when reading aloud. Redirect as necessary.

40. Speak and read clearly, in a normal tone, and at a moderate pace.

41. Rephrase the content areas when reviewing lectures.

42. Do not provide lengthy explanations.

43.   Provide an outline and vocabulary list in written format before introducing new material. Practice reading the words aloud. Encourage the student to preview the information at home before the lesson is presented.

44.   Present new vocabulary words in sentences instead of in isolation. Many words look similar to lip readers.

45.   If the student seems confused with verbal directions, repeat and summarize the information or provide a written copy.

46.   If the student reads lips, a swivel chair is beneficial. The student will be able to see the teacher and the interpreter at all times.

47.   If a student uses hearing devices and seems to be having difficulty, contact the hearing specialist. Often hearing aids need to be tested and adjusted.

Students with Visual Impairments

If a student with visual impairments appears to be inattentive and looking around the classroom, the student may be relying on the auditory channel to obtain information. Students with visual impairments often experience visual fatigue during classroom assignments and may need to rest their eyes.

Various materials are available specifically for visually impaired students. The vision consultant may order enlarged textbooks, magnifiers, closed-circuit television, and computer software with enlarged fonts and pictures. If the student is required to use special technology, you will receive instructions about how to use the equipment. This training is very important so that you are able to assist the student when the specialist is not available.

48.   Provide audiocassettes for the student's use. If the recordings are made in-house, the audiocassettes should be recorded on cassette players with variable recording speeds, enabling the student to increase the speed as auditory skills are refined.

49.   Allow extra time for the student to complete assignments. Be aware of visual fatigue during classroom activities. Some signs of visual fatigue may include red eyes, rubbing of the eyes, laying the head on the desk, and squinting. Discuss with the supervising teacher the types of modifications that should be implemented if the student experiences extreme visual fatigue. One possibility is to allow some of the assignments to be completed orally. If the assignment is completed orally, write a note on the blank assignment page indicating that it was completed orally, and then initial and date it. The general education teacher or parent can contact you should questions arise.

50.   When directing questions to a student with a visual impairment, address the student by name. Often students with visual impairments do not respond to body language, gestures, and/or subtle visual clues due to their low vision.

51.   Tape-record daily assignments. The student may listen to them as many times as needed. This is simple to do and it will foster independence.

52.   Touch is important for visually impaired students. Provide hands-on experiences whenever possible.

Notes

"Children are like wet cement. Whatever falls on them will leave an impression."
-Haim Ginott

Chapter 10

Daily Assignments

The principle reason for daily assignments is to verify the students' understanding of a specific concept or to practice a newly acquired skill. More often than not, students are asked demonstrate their understanding in a written format. For the typical student, this is often a simple task. The student is able to complete the assignment quickly and move on to other projects or perhaps get a head start on daily homework assignments. This is not always true for the student with special needs. Although learning-disabled students have average to above-average intelligence, a student may require additional time to complete an assignment due the reading level or the written language skills required. The student who needs additional time to complete assignments is frequently behind and usually spends a large portion of the school day trying to "catch up" to the other students. The student with special needs frequently falls into this category and often has numerous incomplete assignments, as there simply isn't enough time during the class period to finish the work.

When making instructional modifications to daily assignments, the first step is to determine the objective of the assignment. For this reason, it is important to be in the classroom when the class assignment is given. Once the objective is determined, the assignment can be modified accordingly. For the student who is falling behind and unable to complete the assignment during the allotted class time, it may be appropriate to modify the assignment. Let's look at two hypothetical situations.

Situation #1: The classroom teacher assigns thirty double-digit multiplication problems to the class. The math problems must be transferred from the textbook to paper. The student has copied and completed fourteen of the problems. Upon close examination of the completed problems, you notice the student has made several reversal errors when copying the problems to the notebook paper. After checking the student's answers with a calculator, it is noted that the student achieved 80%. Given this scenario, is it necessary for the student to complete all thirty problems when he has demonstrated that the first fourteen are correct? Probably not, since the objective of the lessons was to demonstrate knowledge of double-digit multiplication.

Situation #2: In English class the students are required to demonstrate knowledge of the subject and predicate of a sentence. The assignment is to divide the model sentence and rewrite the subject in Column 1 and the predicate in Column 2. The student is struggling with rewriting every sentence. Would it be appropriate for the student to draw a line between the subject and predicate in the example instead of rewriting it? Would it be appropriate for the student to complete it orally and use the time for you to reteach or to finish some incomplete assignments that must be turned in the following day?

If these were actual situations, it would be important to check with the supervising teacher before a final decision is made. Most likely, in both situations the supervising teacher would concur that if the student has demonstrated mastery (which is usually 80%), an appropriate use of the remaining class period would be to help the student in other academic areas.

The student with special needs often requires extra support and modifications. The difficulty with the extra support is finding the time during the school day to provide the additional service. Frequently, students with special needs receive additional service during periods which are considered non-academic by the supervising teacher. When this occurs time and again, the student with special needs often considers the supplementary help a punishment instead of support. Therefore, it is important, when possible, to schedule additional academic support during the academic class periods. While students are completing daily assignments, it is an optimum time for the student to receive supplementary remedial support. Therefore, in conjunction with the supervising teacher, it is important to determine the appropriateness of the daily assignments. Ask "Is this beneficial to the student?" and "Is it important for the student to complete the entire assignment if the student is able to demonstrate mastery when completing 50% of the assignment?" Often, daily assignments can be completed orally in half the amount of time, allowing extra time for remediation in other academic areas. If the assignment can be modified, independent work periods can be used to reinforce previously taught skills or help the student complete some of the assignments that cannot be modified. There may be times when other students in the classroom setting will also benefit from reteaching or reinforcement of an activity. The classroom teacher may ask you to include these students within your group.

The following section provides ideas for the modification of daily assignments. Additional ideas and strategies may also be found under the specific subject areas.

53.   Modify the length of the assignment by dividing the assignment in half and assigning only the even or odd problems.

54. Divide the assignment into smaller segments, and complete the assignment over a period of several days.

55. Use a cover sheet when completing long assignments. The assignment may not seem so overwhelming to the student. The cover sheet can also be used to block out distracting stimuli on the page.

56. Allow students to work with partners or in cooperative groups. One member of the group can read the questions aloud while another writes the answers.

57. Allow the student to respond verbally into a tape recorder. The answers can be transcribed at a later time.

58. If the student does not have a consumable textbook, provide a photocopy of the material. Ask the student to highlight, underline, or fill in the blanks on the photocopy instead of copying the entire page of sentences, paragraphs, or math problems.

59. Assignment sheets will help the student organize and prioritize daily assignments. The assignment sheets should include the due date of each assignment. (Be sure the student knows the difference between the words *Do* and *Due* when copying assignments.) Ask the student to check off the assignment when complete. Form #18 and Form #19 in Appendix A may be reproduced for student use.

60. When a student falls behind, allow the student to respond orally while you write the verbatim response. This is beneficial for the student who is continually behind due to difficulty with fine motor control. Be sure the student continues to write some assignments on a daily basis.

61. Allow extra time for completion of assignments.

62. If conducive to the assignment, allow the student to illustrate the answer instead of responding in a written format.

63. Offer supplementary materials that coincide with the text but are at a lower reading level. Look in the teacher's guide. Often textbook companies provide extra blackline masters for different levels: beginning, intermediate, extension, extra practice, and language activities for ESL students. Some of the supplemental material may be appropriate for the student.

64. Provide parallel activities at an appropriate level. For example, if the class objective is to locate nouns in sentences on a worksheet and the student is unable to read the worksheet, the student's reading textbook could be used instead. Allow the student to write the nouns from a story. If the student is unable to read, locate objects in the classroom that are nouns.

65.   General education teachers frequently provide written contracts for individual units. The contract allows for simple modification of the length of the unit by highlighting assignments the student is responsible for completing. Most contracts include the required information and also often include supplemental material which is related to the unit. If the contract includes supplemental "fun" activities, be sure the student has the opportunity to periodically participate in these activities.

66.   Supply the student with a pad of Post-It™ notes. If an assignment is not completed during class time a note is written and is placed into the student's assignment book. When the assignment is complete, the student discards the Post-It™ note.

67.   Use the technology available in the school. Computers, word processors, and calculators will help some students complete the required work.

"Thought is the blossom; language the bud; action is the fruit behind it."
-Ralph Waldo Emerson

Chapter 11

Written Language

Written language is a complex process. Students may encounter difficulty with written language for many different reasons. Students may have trouble formulating and organizing their ideas on paper. While other students in the classroom are busy filling their paper with ideas, this student may simply stare at the paper, unsure of how to sequence the ideas or organize his thoughts. Some students encounter difficulty with the grammar and syntax of written language, whereas others have expressive language limitations and are unable to find the words needed to express themselves. Reluctant writers may not want to write, as, more often than not, their papers are returned covered with corrections. The student may be discouraged and feel it is not worth the time or the effort. A small number of students experience difficulty with fine motor control and may be unable to write within the lines of the standard-size classroom paper. These students may be allowed to use the computer for some activities but still should be required to complete pencil and paper tasks daily to develop the skill. Due to one or several of the previous limitations, you will encounter reluctant writers. It is important to encourage all attempts, no matter how small, and place the emphasis on the students' ideas instead of the sentence structure and spelling.

Another question which frequently arises is whether or not a student should be able to print or is required to write in cursive. With cursive writing, some of the spatial difficulties related to writing are eliminated as the letters are continuous and connected to one another. Letter reversal may also be eliminated with cursive writing. Once a student becomes fluent with cursive writing, it is often faster and easier for him. Some students may be allowed to print, others may be required to learn cursive writing, and some may use a combination of both. The appropriate method will be determined by the special education team.

Prewriting Stage

A large discrepancy exists between some students' writing and that of their peers. Some students may be in a prewriting stage. If the student is in a prewriting stage, parallel or supplemental activities can be provided according to the student's Individualized Education Plan. Many of these activities can also be used to reinforce prereading skills.

68.   Practice letter formation with the use of any of the following materials. The emphasis for this activity may be placed on sound/symbol association, as many of the practice activities can be used with letters. It is important to vary the activities to maintain a high level of interest.

Pudding: Prepare the pudding and pour into a cake pan. The student writes his letters in the pudding and, after writing the letter, the student is able to clean his fingers by licking them. Practice both capital (upper) and lower case letters. Check with the supervising teacher to determine whether to use the word *capital* or *upper case* so the student is learning the same terminology in all settings.

Commercially colored sand, chalk, or salt: Although not as much fun as pudding, these materials work equally well for the student.

Finger-paints: Students love finger-painting. Often this is not the chosen method as it is quite messy. With finger-paints, the student spreads the paint on a piece of glossy paper and then proceeds to write the letters in the paint, saying the letter name while writing. This may be done on a desktop or an easel.

Pipe Cleaners: The students bend a pipe cleaner into letter shapes. The student may trace around the pipe cleaner once the letter is formed.

Playdough or clay: While saying the letter aloud, the student molds the letter with clay or playdough.

Magnetic Letters: Provide the student with a set of capital and lower case letters. Ask the student to match the lower case letter to the corresponding capital letter.

69.   Use commercially purchased tracing paper and ask the student to trace large objects from a coloring book.

If a student is unable to trace, draw the outline with pencil and have the student trace your example with crayon. Once the student becomes proficient with tracing bold outline shapes change the original design to short lines and, finally, small dots. Another option is to enlarge pictures or cartoons with an overhead projector and allow students to trace and color the pictures.

70.   Ask the student to reproduce simple shapes from a model. Use simple pictures from art instruction books, learn-to-draw books, or preschool coloring books.

71.   Make alphabet puzzles. Create an 8 ½" x 11" letter template on tag board. Make two copies of the letter. Keep one as a model and cut the other into 2-4 pieces depending on the ability level of the student. The student can place the pieces on the model to recreate the letter or put the puzzle together without the template. Store the puzzle pieces in individual envelopes.

72.   Allow the student to work with dot-to-dot pictures. Use A, B, C pictures for prereading practice and 1, 2, 3 pictures for math.

        Special activities may be created for additional practice for each letter of the alphabet. Some sample activities are listed on Form #20 Appendix A.

73.   Allow the student to illustrate his response instead of writing the answer.

74.   Ask the special education teacher if letter templates are available. The tracing of templates helps to develop fine motor control.

75.   Inquire whether commercially made paper with raised lines is available. This paper works well to practice letter formation as the raised lines will help to guide the student.

76.   Allow the student to dictate a story to you or a peer. Later, the student can practice reading the story and tracing the letters.

77.   Provide the student with material to copy from a close-up model. As the student becomes more proficient, he may copy from the board or the overhead. The final outcome for the student may be a handwriting goal.

78.   Incorporate other fine motor developmental activities such as stringing beads, making pegboard designs, using sewing cards, weaving, cutting, or using clay during the written language blocks.

One Word at a Time
        When a student has developed some proficiency with fine motor control it is time to begin some initial written language activities. The following ideas are presented for students who are working with individual words and progressing to four to five words joined. Some students may need to copy the words from a model while others may be able to write the words on their own.

79.   Students may begin to label items with one word. Following are some examples of ideas that can be incorporated with labeling.

- The student cuts out and pastes random pictures onto a large piece of construction paper. The student dictates the word for the label and then copies it onto the paper from a model.

- The student selects a category such as food, animals, or toys. The student looks for pictures and pastes them onto construction paper or creates a small book. The pictures are then labeled.

- The student draws a picture of an animal or person. The student labels the body parts.

80. Create a word train with small milk cartons. For this activity the student selects a category such as "smell". The topic is taped to the outside of the milk carton. The student lists words which relate to the topic smell such as skunk, onion, rotten, flowers, etc. If the student is unable to write the words alone, create a word bank, and have the student copy the words onto sentence strips. Cut the sentence strips apart and place them into the milk container. Later these words may be used to write sentences or incorporated into short paragraphs with one topic sentence.

81. Sentence completion activities may also be used. In this activity, sentences that have one word missing are provided to the students. The student fills in the blank. You may provide a choice of two words to insert in the blank, provide a word bank, or, if the student is ready, allow the student to fill in the blank with whatever word he would like, as long as it makes sense.

Beginning Writers

Some students have difficulty generating ideas and may need additional prompts and visual aids to get started. This section includes some ideas to help the reluctant writer.

82. Journal writing is frequently used; as it is not a graded form of writing, there is little risk-taking involved for the reluctant writer. Several types of journal writing are listed here.

- Question-and-answer journal. With this method, a question is written to the student and the student responds in writing. The student directs a question back to the adult.

- Free-response journal. With free response, the student selects and writes freely about a topic. In conjunction with the special education teacher, an individual goal is determined for the student. The goal may range from writing individual words or a single sentence, or to filling an entire page.

- Assigned topics. Assigned topics may take various forms. A picture, an object, or perhaps a fill-in-the-blank sentence is provided for the student, and the student responds with one or two sentences.

83.   Sequence cards will help the student who is unable to generate ideas alone. Provide the students with a sequence of pictures. (If not available in the classroom, these cards may be available from the Speech and Language clinician). The student places the cards in sequential order and writes one or more sentences about each picture. If this is too difficult, discuss the first few pictures in the sequence, and ask student to write a sentence about the final picture card only. As the student becomes more proficient, he may write about the final two cards and so forth.

If sequence cards are not available, look through the comic section of the newspaper. At times you may be able to find cartoons with clear pictures that contain 3-5 picture frames. The frames may be cut apart and used in the same format as sequence cards.

84.   Riddles that require a short-answer response are often motivating. On an index card, write some simple riddles for the student. On the back of the card, the student may write the answer to the riddle or (if needed) copy the answer from a model. When the work is complete, the student may practice reading the riddle aloud and share the riddle with the class. As he progresses, the student may create his own personal riddles. Some examples of simple riddles may include:

- I am thinking of a season of the year when the leaves change color.

- I am thinking of a word that rhymes with "at" and you can put it on your head.

- I am thinking of an animal that wags his tail and barks.

- I am thinking of an object that you can throw and catch.

85.   Reluctant writers often must begin at the basic level. When a student is ready to begin writing sentences, the use of nouns is a perfect place to start. Use some of the following ideas to get the student started.

Begin with a simple sentence such as the following "I like" sentences and then add to the complexity when the student has mastered the skill.

- I like …….. (dogs, ice cream)
- I don't like……. (peas, work)
- I have a……..(fish, bike)

When student is able to fill in the blanks of some basic sentences, he is able to move on to sentences that require more than one word to complete. Some examples may include:

- I like dogs because................ (they are fun to play with.)
- I like my friend because.......... (she is nice.)
- After school I like to......... (play with my brother.)
- I am happy because........ (I am going to see my grandma.)

Once students are comfortable at this level, they may begin writing their own sentences.

Written Language Assignments

86. Brainstorming helps to promote creative thinking and is often used as a prerequisite to writing activities. There are two simple rules to follow when brainstorming with students. First, there is no right or wrong answer and, second, every answer from a serious idea to an outrageous response is acceptable.

87. Provide detailed instructions for written language assignments. Specific instructions may include the predetermined number of paragraphs or sentences, or the overall length. For example, ask the student to write two good paragraphs. Each paragraph should include a topic sentence with two supporting detailed sentences. Gradually decrease the structure as the student becomes more confident in his or her ability to write.

88. Allow the student to choose one familiar idea. Brainstorm to generate a word bank. The word bank will help the student spell the words that he would like to use and also will help to generate ideas. Once the brainstorming session is over, the words can be grouped by subtopic. This will assist the student with the organization of ideas and paragraphing. Continue with the same topic for several days.

89. Students who experience difficulty generating ideas may need a list of topics from which to choose. Form #21 in Appendix A includes some possible story starters. The ideas on Form #21 have been divided into subgroups of titles, beginning sentences, and unbelievable excuses. The possibilities are endless. Once the idea is generated, assist with the development of an outline of the story or topic. Forms #22 and #23 may be used to outline the story.

90. Keep a selection of pictures available for students. Pictures from magazines, posters, newspapers, old photos from antique shops, etc., will all help the student to generate ideas.

Concrete examples may also help students generate ideas. Place a common classroom object on the table (pencil, book, bottle of glue, etc.) Have the student write a paragraph beginning with "If I were a bottle of glue, I would…"

91. Ask the student to bring a picture from home and write about the picture. You may want to use the Story Planner – Form #22 in Appendix A.

92. If the student has difficulty generating ideas, request him to write a minimum number of sentences per day. (You may have to start at one!) Build on the topic each day. The next week, increase the goal. Be sure the student is held responsible for meeting the individual goal.

93. If the student is unable to generate a sentence on his own, write descriptive words or illustrate the idea. The words may be combined into simple sentences at a later time.

94. Write the student's ideas on paper and ask him to recopy the sentences from the model.

The Writing Process

95. Avoid excessive corrections of the mechanical aspects of writing, especially when a student is beginning to write. Focus on the development of ideas.

96. Visual organizers are useful for students to help define characters, to organize thoughts, to compare and contrast ideas, and even to expand vocabulary. The map should include the key ideas and words relating to the topic. Mapping also helps the student to visualize the relationship between the parts of the story.

The following example illustrates how to use mapping when writing a simple paragraph. The topic, "Dogs" is written into the center. The paper is then divided into four sections. In each section the student writes words that pertain to some aspect of the dog. In this example, the topics include feeding, exercising, grooming, and training dogs as pets. When the mapping exercise is complete, the student uses the words to develop sentences or paragraphs. The story is organized for the student. In this example, the student has a main topic, four paragraphs, and a selection of key words for each paragraph.

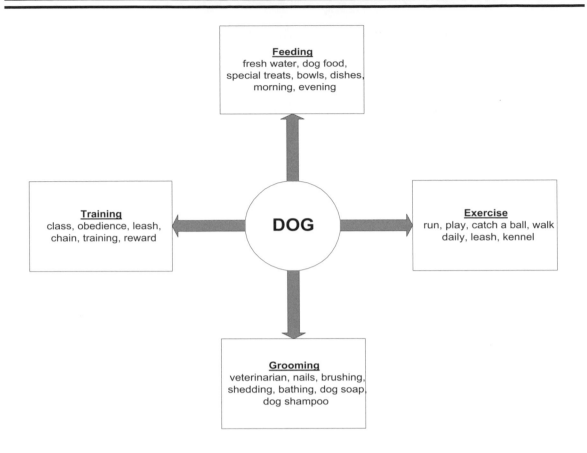

Mapping may also be used to help students increase their vocabularies. Following is an example of an antonym web map.

Antonym Web

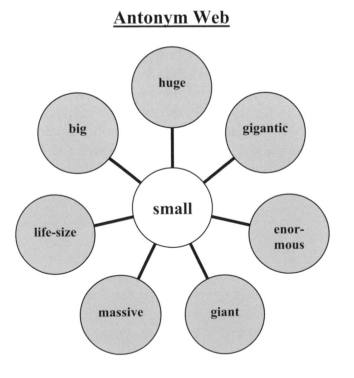

Story characters may also be mapped out. For a character map, the character would be listed in the center circle and the individual characteristics may be listed in the surrounding circles.

97.　Before the student begins to write a story, have the student answer the following questions:

- Who is the main character?
- Who else is in the story?
- What does the main character want to do in the story?
- What happens when the main character does this?
- How does the story end?

These simple questions will help students with the organization of their thoughts and with making an outline for the story. Photocopy Form #22 or #23 from Appendix A.

98.　Teach the importance of a beginning, middle, and end to paragraphs. Incorporate transition words such as *first*, *next*, *then*, *last*, or *finally* when writing paragraphs. Transition words help students to sequence their thoughts.

Transition words for more advanced writers may include *accordingly*, *also*, *besides, furthermore, lastly, nevertheless, otherwise, since, therefore*, and *thus*.

99.　Help the student discover the importance of proofing all assignments. Provide a checklist form for proofreading. The form should include the following: capitalization, punctuation, spelling, paragraph indentation, margins, and sentence sense. The form is used as follows: The student reads the entire paper and edits the paper for capital letters. When completed, the student checks capitalization off on the form. The second time, the student reads and edits the paper for punctuation. Continue in this manner until the entire paper is proofread. Form #24 in Appendix A includes several samples which may be photocopied.

100.　The SPACE strategy may be used as an error-monitoring strategy when proofreading writing. The acronym SPACE stands for the following:

Spelling
Punctuation
Appearance　　　　Sara **P**icks **A**pples **C**arefully **E**very **A**fternoon
Capitalization
Error Analysis

The student can select the format which is the easiest to remember. Practice using the SPACE technique with written language assignments.

101. Ask the student to read his story aloud or tape record the story once complete. Many students are able to hear erroneous sentence construction even though visually they may not see it on their paper. It is important when using this method that the student read the assignment exactly as it is written and that he does not insert additional words. Allow the student ample time to make the corrections.

102. Since written language is an important form of communication, allow students to share their stories and reports often. It is also important for students to hear good models. You may want to ask students to share their stories and reports or select some samples and read them aloud. If a student does not feel comfortable reading aloud, discuss the situation with the supervising teacher. The student may feel more comfortable sharing the story if allowed time to practice reading the story prior to sharing.

103. Use a computer or a word processor for some of the written language assignments. Most schools teach keyboarding at a young age. Older students will be able to use the computer to check their spelling and grammar, and to use the thesaurus.

104. Some students may not be able to produce long written assignments; therefore, it may be more important in some cases to look at the quality of the assignment. When teaching topic sentences, details, and closing sentences, ask the student to produce one quality paragraph instead of a series of multiple, hastily written paragraphs.

105. When working on class reports, some students may need to use a fill-in-the-blank format. These can easily be created for any topic. At the elementary level, an example for the topic *Birds* might be:

My bird is a _____. He lives in the _____ part of the United States. He is _____ in color.

The student can add as many details as required.

106. When writing research papers, students will need assistance with the formulation of topic sentences and with a simple outline if needed. Encourage the student to look for the details in his reading. Using the topic of Lions, some topic sentences may include:

- The lion is a member of the cat family. (The student adds details).

- The lion can be found in many countries throughout the world. (The student lists the various countries or regions).

- The lion is a carnivore. (The student lists the food sources).

For the student who has difficulty reading, you may also want to modify the number of sources in the bibliography.

107.   If a student has difficulties organizing his thoughts on paper, ask him to write the first draft on lined notebook paper, skipping several spaces between each sentence. When this is complete, the student cuts the sentences into strips and physically organizes the sentences. Form #25 in Appendix A includes some sample sentences for the student to practice this technique. Also included are templates which may be reproduced for individual students.

108.   Allow the student to present the final project to the class in an alternative format. A videotape, demonstration, display, or oral presentation may capitalize on the student's strengths.

Spelling in the Context of Written Language Assignments

109.   At first glance, a written language assignment with numerous spelling errors may appear to lack creativity and solid ideas. Beginning writers should be allowed to spell phonetically. Ask the student to read his response to you. Revise the paper with the student. Give encouragement to all attempts.

110.   Choose one or more frequently used words from the student's journal or creative writing assignments. Develop a spelling dictionary of frequently misspelled words. Encourage the student to use the dictionary and thesaurus when proofreading assignments.

Fine Motor Skills

Students with special needs are often very creative. A delay in fine motor skills may cause difficulty and frustration for the student when transferring the ideas to paper. Instead of allowing the creativity to flow, the student may write in short, choppy sentences to compensate for the difficulty with fine motor control. Interestingly, when the obstacle of writing is removed, many of these students are among the most creative writers.

111.   Ask the special or general education teacher to model a correct pencil grip. Check the student's pencil grip. Place adhesive tape or a commercially bought pencil grip on the pencil.

112.   Some students are unable to write within the lines of the suggested grade-level paper. If you are working at the upper grades wider ruled paper may be secured from primary level teachers. Students who have difficulty writing within the lines should begin with the wide ruled size and slowly decrease the size until he is using grade-level paper. If the correct size of paper is unavailable commercially, create the appropriate size for the student using lined paper and a felt tipped pen or by using the computer. Photocopy the paper for future use.

113.   Write the student's answers or dictated story in pencil and ask the student to trace it with a fine-tipped pen.

114.   It is often difficult for students to copy from a distant model, so provide a close-up model if possible. Students frequently lose their place when transferring information from the board to paper, especially if the student is unable to read the material. If the material is written in cursive and the student still prints, you may have to transcribe the material for the student.

115.   Affix an alphabet card or alphabet strip to the student's desk or folder so the student is able to see the correct formation of the letters. Allow the use of manuscript or cursive on daily assignments, depending on the student's preference.

116.   If appropriate, write out long assignments for the student. With long assignments, it may also be permissible for the parent to write the homework assignments for their child. If the expectations are changed, the new expectations will need to be communicated to the parents or guardian.

117.   If available, provide the student with a word processor or a laptop computer to use in completing long assignments.

"Treat people as if they were what they ought to be and you help them become what they are capable of being."
-Goether

Chapter 12

Spelling

Spelling words should be compatible with the reading level of the student. The special education teacher will provide an appropriate list of words if the classroom list is too difficult. As with all modifications, spelling modifications may be simple or complex. Simple modifications may include modifying the length of the list, whereas a complex modification may include the creation of an alternate spelling program.

If the student is not developmentally ready for a formal spelling program, this time may be used to work on additional fine motor activities such as letter formation and sound/symbol relationships.

Grade-Level Spelling Lists

Many students with disabilities are able to succeed in the regular spelling curriculum with minimal modifications. In conjunction with the supervising teacher, you may want to consider some of the following curriculum and instructional modifications.

118.   Often the classroom spelling list is modified by adjusting the number of words on the list. Guidelines will be determined by the special education teacher and also be noted in the IEP.

119.   Increase the student's goal when the mastery level is met on three consecutive tests. For example, the student may study a list of five words for three weeks. If the student successfully masters the list, the goal may increase to seven words. (Often you will be the person responsible for tracking the student progress and advising the supervising teacher when the goal has been met.)

120.   At the beginning of the school year, create a master copy of all of the spelling units. The student will be able to study the words in advance, and if the student forgets the weekly spelling list, the comprehensive list is at home.

121.   Often, spelling words can be grouped into word families. Word families are groups of words that have similar endings. By learning the most common word families (see Form #26 in Appendix A), the student will be able to spell many different words. The student should begin with simple word patterns that have only one vowel such as –at. By learning this simple word pattern students will be able to spell the following simple words: bat, cat, fat, hat, mat, pat, rat, and sat. The student is then able to proceed to the patterns with more vowels and combinations of consonants.

When teaching word families, introduce one word family to the student and practice using the pattern before moving on. For example, on Monday, introduce the word family "at." On Tuesday, review the word family "at" and practice reading the words which were created. If the student clearly recalls the previous lesson a second word family may be introduced.

Use letter squares from the game Scrabble™ to reinforce spelling with students. Index cards may also be used. Write the word family pattern on the index card and make individual cards for the initial consonant sounds. The student can manipulate the initial consonant sounds to make new words.

122.   If the student is unable to read the spelling list, delete some of the unfamiliar words. Insert commonly used sight words or pattern words that correspond to the current lesson. Ask the special education teacher for an appropriate list of sight words. Form #27 includes the 100 most common words in the English language. Words 1-25 on the list make up about one-third of all printed material so this is a good place to start. The first one hundred words make up almost half of all written material. This list was adapted from *The Reading Teacher's Book of Lists*, Fourth Edition, ©2000, which includes the 1000 most commonly used words in the English language. For more information on this book, see Appendix B.

123.   If the student is unable to use the current grade-level spelling list, the computer may be used to adapt a previous grade-level list to a similar format used in the classroom.

Parallel Spelling Activities

Not all students are developmentally ready for a formalized spelling program. Some students may need parallel activities. These activities may be completed alone, with a peer, or with you.

124.   Create a spelling list of initial letter sounds that coincide with the initial letters of the class spelling list. The student can simultaneously work on the sound/symbol relationships and letter formation while the other students continue with the class

spelling list. During the assessment the student can write the initial consonant sound as peers write the entire word. An example would be:

Class	Student
store	s
book	b
take	t

Due to the irregular sounds of words beginning with vowels, there will be times when additional words may need to be substituted. Once the student has mastered the initial consonant sounds, he may proceed to the final consonants.

125.   Start with basic sight words and simple phonetic words such as *a, at, am,* and *an* when the student is able to reproduce several letter sounds consistently. Form #26 lists common word families and column one on Form #27 lists some common sight words which may be incorporated.

126.   A simple spelling list may also be created by using the student's proper name with several simple sight words. Once the spelling list is created, simple sentences may be developed (written language activity), or the activity may also be used to practice letter formation (fine motor and handwriting activity). An example would be:

- Weekly spelling list: Mary, my, is, name
- Written language sentences: My name is Mary. Mary is my name.

Once the student has mastered the initial list, names of additional family members, friends, peers, or pets can be added.

127.   Provide supplemental practice pages of the words. The student may trace the words with multiple colors of crayons, felt-tipped pens, or fine-tip markers. This approach is good for students who have difficulty learning sounds and who need a whole word method. It also alleviates the frustration of practicing and learning a word incorrectly.

128.   Provide practice sheets the student can trace. Use peers to drill and monitor the student's progress.

Drill and Practice Activities

Drill and practice activities take place daily in the classroom. The student may practice alone, with a peer, or with an adult.

129.   Group words that contain common prefixes and suffixes. The prefix is added at the beginning of a word and the suffix at the end. Teach the spelling and meaning of the prefixes, suffixes, and base words in isolation. Form #28 in Appendix A contains a list of common prefixes and suffixes and their meanings.

130. To help students visually discriminate between the various parts of the word, use three different colors to highlight the syllables. For example, highlight the base word with yellow, the prefix with green, and the suffix with blue to aid with visual discrimination.

131. Reinforce only one spelling rule at a time. Form #29 in Appendix A includes some basic phonetic rules that will help students with both spelling and reading. Although not fully inclusive, it will provide some general guidelines.

132. Provide a close-up model from which to work. Many students experience difficulty when copying unknown words from a distant model.

133. Combine spelling and handwriting goals to allow time for extra drill and practice.

134. When practicing spelling words, plan for a minimum of ten minutes structured practice time. Students who experience difficulty with organizational skills will need this time to find and organize their materials.

135. Do not require all students to practice all words daily. This may be too overwhelming for some. Practice two or three words daily if the student is frustrated by a long list.

136. Make supplemental drill and practice exercises such as spelling bingo, hangman, and word finds.

137. Vary the daily drill and practice exercises. Along with paper and pencil tasks, allow daily practice on the chalkboard, in small groups, orally, or with a tape recorder.

138. For younger students, practice spelling words with shaving cream, sand trays, finger-paints, or pudding.

139. Provide an audiocassette of the word list. To save time, record the pretest while the general education teacher administers it. Once the list is recorded the student can practice alone, during extra class time, or at home. This audiocassette may also be used if a student needs to retest or was absent during the regular testing session.

140. Make rainbow words. Make word strips with the spelling words. The student traces the word with several different color markers or crayons. This will provide drill and practice for correct letter formation. Trace each word with three or four colors.

141. Allow the student to practice on a typewriter, computer, or word processor.

142. Assist students with configuration clues to recall correct spelling.

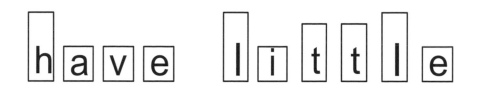

Study Methods for Spelling

For students with disabilities, the most effective method is one that will capitalize on the student's strengths. Three guidelines for studying spelling words are listed here. Allow the student to experiment with the various spelling study methods. The student will be able to choose a study method that best meets his individual needs. Practice the method several times until the student is proficient with the selected study method. Spot-check the student's work frequently if he is practicing alone. Form #30 in Appendix A includes a checklist for each method. These checklists may be reproduced for the student.

Visual Learners

143. This read-and-spell method focuses on the student's visual strength. This method is appropriate for students with hearing impairments or students who rely on visual patterning.

- The student views the word while you read it aloud. (Provide the student with a flashcard.)
- The student studies the word by reading it aloud, spelling it aloud, and then reading it again.
- The student attempts to spell the word orally two times without looking at the card.
- If the student is able to spell the word correctly, he attempts to write the word without a model.

Auditory Learners

144. The hear-and-spell method relies heavily on auditory skills to learn new words. The following steps may be implemented into the spelling program. This method should also be used for the student with a visual impairment.

- The student observes while the word is written on a flashcard, the blackboard, or the overhead projector.
- The student reads the word and repeats the letters verbally after the teacher.
- Once again, the student listens to the teacher spell the word and repeats it after the teacher.
- The student spells the word aloud without assistance.

Multisensory Approach

145.   The cover-and-write method is appropriate for a student who needs a multisensory approach.

- The student looks at the word and pronounces it. (Provide flashcards with individual sample words. Students may make their own cards, but the cards should be checked for accuracy before the student begins the practice session.)
- The student covers the card or turns it over and spells the word aloud without looking at it.
- The student writes the word while viewing the model.
- The student compares the word to the model.
- If the word is written correctly, the student practices writing the word three additional times.
- A final check is made. If the word is correct, the student practices the next word.

Spelling Tests
Many students with disabilities not only need to learn to spell the word, but also to read the word.

146.   If a student has difficulty with writing, test him orally outside of the classroom, preferably while the others are taking their test.

147.   Have the student spell the word orally. Write the response verbatim. This provides assistance to the student experiencing fine motor difficulty.

148.   Cue the student as to the number of letters in each word when working with silent letters. This helps the phonetic speller to include the silent letters.

149.   Test several words daily in place of one final test.

150.   With lower functioning students, allow the students to select corresponding spelling flashcards for word recognition.

151.   If the student needs long periods of time to process information and you are unable to administer the test individually, create an audiocassette. The student will be able to stop the tape and think about the word for as long as needed.

152.   If letters are frequently reversed, ask the student to spell the word orally when correcting the test. Give credit for each correct response.

Grading

In all instances, the supervising teacher is responsible for selecting grading criteria. You may be asked to keep a record of scores. Some techniques that may be used follow:

153.   Record pretest and posttest scores. Give these scores to the classroom teacher. The teacher may base the student's grade on effort and improvement instead of percentiles.

154.   Ask students to self monitor their spelling progress by creating a chart of their pretest and posttest scores. Often students are motivated by self-monitoring techniques.

155.   Set a weekly goal. Reward the student if the individual goal is met. All struggling students need encouragement.

Notes

A man has one hundred dollars and you leave him with two-that's subtraction."
–Mae West

Chapter 13

Mathematics

Mathematics is often considered a second language – the language of symbols. Therefore the difficulties a student experiences in mathematics may be directly related to processing of information. Students who have difficulty with letter reversals may also have difficulty with number reversals. Auditory and visual processing, sequencing of steps, and rote memory may also cause difficulty for individual students. Mathematics often requires a process of sequential steps to produce the correct answer. Confusion may result if the student has difficulty with sequencing, as the student may forget one step of the process. Frequently, when analyzing a student's work, this is the origin of the problem. Since math concepts build upon previously learned concepts, the student who is unsure of basic addition, subtraction, or multiplication facts will have a difficult time with long division problems and more advanced math. In this case, the student errors may not occur in the actual process but may be the result the student's inability to recall the basic math facts.

With basic math, students with disabilities often require the use of concrete materials such as manipulatives so they are able to better understand the abstract concepts. Frequently, the supervising teacher will use manipulatives when demonstrating a concept to the class. Some students may also need manipulatives for daily assignments. Other students may have difficulty using manipulatives with assignments due to the multiple steps involved. For example, when using concrete material as an aid, the student must first complete the operation using the concrete materials. Once the student obtains an answer, he must retain the answer his short-term memory in order to transfer the answer to paper. Since many students with disabilities also have difficulty with short-term memory, this is no easy task. Therefore, when working with students in mathematics, you may need to try several methods and options before finding one that works well with the individual student. The supervising teacher will provide training with the manipulatives, and you will learn a great deal simply by observing the teacher during instruction.

When providing service in the math setting, refer to the chapters entitled Daily Assignments and Assessment. Both chapters have many practical ideas to support the student in the area of math.

General Teaching Strategies

156.   Students with disabilities may experience difficulty with abstract concepts. Point out how math is really a part of daily life. Reinforcing math concepts in "real life" situations brings meaning and helps students understand the relevance of mathematics. Examples of real life situations include telling time, measuring sound, understanding budgets, calculating discounts on sale items, balancing a checkbook, counting calories, cooking, reading a bus schedule, determining the amount of rainfall, etc. When working on a skill, try to personalize the concept and explain to the student why it is necessary to learn.

157.   When monitoring students, do not worry about perfect math calculations. Look for their understanding of the process. Once the process is understood, check the accuracy of the calculations. Limit the number of practice problems to 7-10 per lesson.

158.   Reinforce key math terms separately. Provide students with a dictionary of math terms taken directly from the math textbook. Help the student to create drawings and step-by-step examples to illustrate the various concepts.

159.   Use drawings, diagrams, and visual demonstrations to help the student establish the relationship between the concrete and the abstract. When problem-solving is involved, encourage the student to illustrate the possible solutions.

160.   Use colored chalk or fine-tip markers when reinforcing assignments. Direct the student's attention to the important points. Color-code the groups of ones, tens, and hundreds, or color-code the columns of numbers to help with regrouping.

161.   Highlight the similar math operations on each page. Highlight all addition problems in yellow, subtraction in blue, and so forth. If the assignment includes several types of math calculations (i.e., addition and subtraction) on one page, the student should complete all the addition problems before proceeding to the subtraction problems.

162.   Teach math fact families. Show the student the relationships between numbers. An example of a math fact family follows:

$$6 + 4 = 10 \qquad 10 - 4 = 6$$
$$4 + 6 = 10 \qquad 10 - 6 = 4$$

163.   If applicable, model math problems using manipulatives. The special or general education teacher can teach you the correct procedure. When modeling, explain each step verbally. Then instruct the student to verbalize each step to you, while practicing the procedure. Listen carefully. You will be able to understand the thinking process used and analyze which step is causing difficulty for the student. Patterns of errors usually emerge in the following areas: inadequate knowledge of facts, incorrect operations, or use of ineffective strategies.

164.   When using number lines to reinforce concepts, make a large number line on the floor for the student to walk on. This assists the student with directionality. If a student is unable to grasp the number line concept, use counters, cubes, popsicle sticks, or buttons for reinforcement.

165.   When teaching the concept of money, use real money instead of paper or cardboard money.

166.   Test a student individually if the class is using timed tests. Reduce the number of problems or increase the time limit. Make sure the student has extra paper to diagram or draw pictures if the basic facts are not memorized. An alternative to timed tests is to use the computer. In many commercial math programs, a specific amount of time and number of problems may be preset. If using timed tests, ask the student to graph his results. Encourage the student to look for improvement. Some classroom teachers insist on timed tests, although for students with disabilities the most frequent outcome of timed-tests is frustration.

167.   When reinforcing word problems, simplify the vocabulary. Often, word problems include irrelevant information. Discuss why the information is irrelevant. Cross it out. Teach key words that are associated with word problems. When reinforcing word problems, it is helpful to ask the student to do the following:

 • Read the problem and determine the question.

 • Reread the word problem. Look for key words in the problem. Some of the key words are: altogether, together, in all, are left, spent, or remain.

 • Draw a picture of the word problem.

 • Write out the problem. Estimate the answer before solving it. If the answer seems reasonable, solve the problem.

Parallel Math Activities

Some students are unable to complete the same curriculum as the rest of the class. For these students, it is important to be aware of the goals and objectives written in the Individualized Educational Plan. Supplementary skills that correspond with the class activity can be provided in the classroom. Listed below are just a few activities that can be completed with the student.

168. Provide parallel activities in the same content areas as those used by the rest of the class. For example, if the class is learning addition with regrouping, the student may work on basic addition facts. It is possible the student can still be involved in the discussion and demonstration; and use the same manipulatives.

169. Correlate the objectives from the Individualized Education Plan with the instruction. If the student is working on number recognition, use daily assignments or the textbook to find numbers. If the objective is number formation, the student can copy problems from the textbook.

170. Use dot-to-dot activities for number sequencing and number recognition.

171. Work on number formation with the use of tracers or templates.

172. Provide the student with number cards. Work on the chronological sequencing of numbers. The same cards may be used for one-to-one correspondence, ordering from least to greatest, and number recognition.

173. Make cards for numbers and mathematical symbols. Have the student put them together into correct mathematical equations. The student may copy the equations onto paper.

174. Collect shells, beads, seeds, various shaped pastas, and buttons. Put them into boxes or bags. Use these collections to sort and classify objects. The materials may also be used to assist with one-to-one correspondence.

175. Use egg cartons to sort materials and to establish the concept of group. The concept of a group needs to be established before addition and subtraction can be introduced.

176. Teach the student the functions of a calculator. Allow him to do some of the problems from the classroom textbook with the calculator.

177. The student may collate math papers into chronological order for the class.

178. When providing parallel curriculum, coordinate the student's assessments, seatwork and rewards with the general education math class.

179. Look for corresponding educational games the student can play with other students in the classroom. Vary the peer group.

180. If a computer is available, look for computer programs that include number recognition, counting, matching, dot-to-dot, or sequencing of numbers.

181.   Keep a box of supplemental math materials in the classroom. Activities can be selected daily from the box, and materials can be updated as needed.

Modifying Math Assignments

182.   Place arrows on the student's worksheet to assist with directionality. Many students will try to perform math calculations from left to right instead of right to left, which is required for many math calculations.

183.   Draw dotted lines between columns of math problems so the student is able to record the information in the correct column. Lined paper may also be turned vertically for ready-made columns, or graph paper may be used for instant organization.

184.   Box in the ones column so the student knows where to begin the math calculation.

185.   Check to see if consumable texts are available. Students with fine motor difficulty will not have to copy the problems; therefore, they will be able to spend more time with the actual calculations.

186.   If consumable texts are unavailable, ask permission to photocopy and enlarge the text so the student may write on the photocopied page.

187.   When working with problem-solving activities, emphasize the problem-solving steps, not the final answer. Many students do not participate in problem-solving activities for fear the final computation is incorrect.

188.   Number the steps in word problems. Highlight important words.

189.   Allow the student to use charts, graphs, and tables to complete their assignments once the processes of addition, subtraction, multiplication, and division are understood.

190.   When using addition or multiplication charts, provide the student with a cutout "L." This will assist the student in finding the intersection box of columns and rows.

191.   Allow ample time to memorize the math facts before using the calculator. If a student is able to count by two, five, and ten, he may also learn to count by three, four, six, etc., which will enable him to multiply without the use of a calculator.

Touch Math® is a math program developed by Innovative Learning Concepts. This program provides hands-on learning for students without the use of manipulatives. Touch-points are strategically located on each number and the student counts the points. Students who are able to count both forward and backward can easily learn to add and subtract. The program also uses Touch-points for multiplication and division.

Student Aids

192.   When teaching multiple-step math calculations, provide a visual model next to the written steps. The student will be able to see the correlation between the model and the written problem.

193.   Create a small booklet for the student to keep as a math reference book. The booklet should include the basic math concepts covered in the class. The student can refer to the booklet if confused about a mathematical operation. Include the math terminology and a visual diagram for each step.

194.   Attach a number line to the student's desk. This will assist the student with addition, subtraction, and the correct formation of the numbers. This will also assist students who experience difficulties with number reversals.

195.   Teach the student how to use the face clock in the classroom as a counting tool for addition and subtraction facts to 12. This will support the student who is adverse to having a number line placed on the desk.

196.   Create a chart with two number lines. Label one for addition with an arrow to the right and label the other chart for subtraction with an arrow running to the left. This will help the student to internalize the concept.

197.   Allow the student to use rubber number stamps if number formation is extremely difficult.

198.   Use stick-on notes to help the student keep his place in the text.

"Our patience will achieve more than our force."
-Edmund Burke

Chapter 14

Organizational Skills

Organizational skills frequently need to be taught to both general and special education students. Simple skills such as keeping pencils and crayons in their proper place, hanging their coats on the coat hook, keeping their personal space organized, and returning items to their proper location should begin as soon as the student enters school. Assignment sheets and homework books may be used as soon as the student begins to have homework. As a student reaches middle school, organization is more complex, as the student may have five to seven class periods and different materials are often needed for each individual class. Frequently, the disorganized student may complete assignments but misplace them; as a result, an assignment is turned in late or may not be turned in at all. As a paraprofessional, you will spend a large amount of time helping students become organized. Some students also will need help with organization of time and physical space.

The book *Winning the Study Game – Learning How to Succeed in School* by Lawrence J. Greene ©2002, listed in Appendix B is highly recommended for students with learning disabilities, those who are at-risk, and Title One students in grades six through eleven who needs a comprehensive study skills program. The readability level of approximately 5.5 allowing students to focus on acquiring the skills needed, without having to struggle with reading the material. The skills in this program may be taught in isolation or used as a comprehensive study skills program with individual students or small groups of students.

Organizing the Environment

199. At the beginning of the school year, some students will benefit from having a simplified map of the school. Highlight the student's classroom areas and include arrows to indicate the most direct route between classes.

200. Many students need to know in advance what is going to occur. If a daily schedule is not posted, create one. This will help the student anticipate what is about to occur. Some students are very dependent upon routine. For these students, changes in the schedule should be discussed early in the day.

201. The majority of classrooms have a specific location where the student turns in daily assignments and homework. Encourage the student to turn in material as soon as he arrives to class. If the location changes frequently, find a peer to help the student.

202. Provide the student with a gentle reminder several minutes before the class period ends. The reminder may be visual such as pointing the clock or a simple oral reminder. Often, disorganized students need several extra minutes to organize their materials before a transition.

203. The student should be seated in a classroom location that allows him to see both the board and the teacher without turning his body. In science labs or classrooms with tables, the student should not have his back to the teacher. If the seating is not conducive to the student's learning, speak with the supervising teacher.

204. For the student who is easily distracted, special seating may also be needed. The student should be seated away from windows, doors, the pencil sharpener, and high traffic areas.

Student Organization

205. Color-code folders for each subject area. If possible, coordinate the folders with the colors of the textbook. A pencil, pen, paper, and other necessary items should be included in each folder.

206. If individual folders are confusing and material is still misplaced, encourage the student to use a three-ring notebook. All of the student folders, papers and the assignment book may be inserted into the three-ring binder. With this method, the student is instructed to keep all assignments in the binder until it is time to turn each one in. Classroom handouts may be three-hole-punched and also inserted into the notebook. At the upper grade levels, students may need two binders. The majority of students are able to go to their lockers during lunch so it may be wise to have one binder for the morning and another one for the afternoon classes.
      In the book *Winning the Study Game* (listed in Appendix B), Lawrence J. Greene recommends the following:

- Buy or make subject dividers to include in the binder.

- Section One of the binder should include the assignment sheet. (You may reproduce Form #18 or Form #19 from Appendix A.)

- Section One should also include a personal study schedule. In *Winning the Study Game,* Greene provides a method for estimating the amount of study time needed for each subject area. This enables students to create their own weekly study schedules. Form #31 is a modified version of a home study schedule. Students may use this form to develop their own personal study schedules. On this schedule students should block out a daily study time. Each student should practice using the schedule and then add additional study time if needed.

- Section Two should include individual tabs for each subject area where all papers may be saved and stored.

- Store all important papers in the binder. Greene suggests a manila envelope should also be 3-hole-punched and inserted into the binder to store important papers.

207. Tape a large manila envelope to the inside of the student's desk. If assignments are not complete, the student can slip the paper into the envelope to complete later.

   For older students provide manila envelopes help keep materials for large projects or assignments with multiple components in one place.

208. Help the student clean and organize his desk or locker at least once a week. Organize the papers into three piles: file into folders, take home, or toss.

209. Make sure the student includes a heading on all papers. With written assignments, it is easy to confuse a social studies rough draft with an English rough draft. Proper headings help the student organize paper into the appropriate folders or sections of the three-ring notebook.

210. Ask students to share their organizational tips. Keep a list of ideas so you can help future students figure out the system that works best for them.

211. Encourage students to use a homework book or an assignment sheet. Help the student learn how to prioritize assignments. Some students need a weekly or monthly calendar to understand the concept of time. Form #32 in Appendix A may be used to rank assignments and calculate the approximate time needed to complete each assignment.

212.   List assignments and the approximate length of time for completion. This will assist the student in prioritizing his class work and managing individual time.

213.   Supply each student with a pad of "Things to Do Today." Ask the students to write reminders to themselves.

214.   Ask a peer to help monitor assignments. The peer may help the student place the assignments into the correct folders.

215.   Allow students who have difficulty remembering to do homework assignments to call home and leave a message on a recorder. Be sure the message includes the subject and the page numbers of the assignment.

216.   Check out an extra set of textbooks for home use. Many times a student will fill in the assignment book but will forget to pack the textbooks.

217.   Create a simple daily checklist to tape on the top of the student's desk or into a notebook. The student may write the assignments with the due dates and cross off each assignment when complete.

218.   When an assignment is complete, encourage the student to turn it in immediately. It can be very frustrating if the student must redo an assignment because it is lost. Special arrangement may need to be made with the classroom teacher.

219.   Plastic bags work well to store extra pencils, crayons, markers, and supplies. At the elementary level, students can keep several individual bags of supplies. When transitioning to another class, the student will not have to search for supplies.

220.   Spot-check students at the beginning and the end of transition times. Many students miss directions because they are organizing their supplies.

221.   If assisting students with check-in and check-out times, go to the student's classroom so that the student will not miss valuable class time or important directions. Form #33 in Appendix A may be reproduced for the student.

222.   Teach the student to use self-talk methods. Ask the student to verbalize the steps, after the teacher has given a multi-step direction.

"Children are likely to live up to what you believe of them."
-Charlotte "Lady Bird" Johnson

Chapter 15

Directions

Every day, students must process hundreds of directions. Many students experience difficulty in school because they are not able to do this processing. Inattention, difficulty with auditory processing, memory deficits, poor listening skills, limited receptive language, and inability to sequence information are only a few of the reasons. No matter what the root of the problem is, it can be a very frustrating experience for the student.

Oral Directions

223. Be sure the student is looking at you before giving directions. Eye contact is important as it signifies that the student is listening.

224. Help students become aware of key words that indicate a series of directions such as *first, second, next, then,* and *finally.*

225. If the general education teacher presents the directions orally, write the directions so the student is able to refer back to them.

226. Do not add irrelevant information during oral directions. Keep directions concise and simple.

227. Simplify the vocabulary. Accompany verbal explanations with visual demonstrations whenever possible.

228.   Divide each direction into one- or two-step components. If the directions are complex, allow the student to complete the first steps before giving additional directions.

229.   Appoint a peer tutor to coach the student through multiple-step directions.

230.   Ask the student to repeat directions back to check for understanding.

231.   Use a combination of visual and auditory directions for the student. When possible, consider drawing pictures of the steps.

232.   Use a camera. Photograph the various steps of experiments, demonstrations, or other multiple-step activities. Glue the pictures in chronological order into a file folder. The student may use this folder as a visual aid. File the directions with the unit for future use.

233.   For the student who continually experiences difficulty with oral directions, practice the skills with the following activities.

Activity #1: Collect various small objects found in the classroom such as a pencil, pen, eraser, paper clip, staple remover, key, and chalk.   Place two dissimilar types of paper (lined, unlined, colored, etc.) on the student's desk.   For this activity, simple one- and two-step directions are given to the student and the student is asked to respond. Ask the student to pay close attention as the direction will not be repeated. As the student becomes proficient, increase to multiple-step directions.

Sample one-step directions:
- Place your pencil in the center of the notebook paper.
- Next, put the paper clip on the red construction paper.
- Now place the key below the paper clip.
- How many objects are on your red construction paper?

Sample two-step directions:
- First, place the staple remover and the chalk in the center of the construction paper.
- Next, put the pencil at the top of the notebook paper and the pen at the bottom.
- Finally, put the key between the pen and pencil and clip the paper clip to the top of the construction paper.

As the student becomes more proficient, increase the number of objects and the complexity of the directions.

Activity #2: For this activity, the student will need a piece of paper and a pencil. Once again, let the student know that the directions will not be repeated so it is important to pay close attention. The activity may also be adapted for any level.

- Write your name in the lower right-hand corner of your paper, and the date in the upper right-hand corner.
- In the center of the paper, place a lower case letter *a*. The lower case letter *a* should be approximately one inch in size.
- Next write a capital *B* in the lower left corner and a capital *C* in the upper right corner.
- Finally, draw a line to connect the three letters. When finished, fold the paper in half and put your pencil down.
- When all students have finished, ask: "What did you draw on the paper?" (a diagonal line)

234. Record daily assignments on tape. This will allow the student to listen to the directions as many times as needed. Include the due dates. Encourage the student to list incomplete assignments into the homework notebook.

235. If the student has a hearing impairment, appoint a peer to cue the student when directions are given orally in class or over the intercom system. Always check for understanding.

Written Directions

236. Provide directions in sequential order. If there are multiple steps, number the steps or place a colored dot between each step of the instructions.

237. Allow extra time to copy the directions for assignments. If the student is unable to copy from a distant model, ask a peer to write or dictate the directions to the student.

238. Ask the student to read written directions at least twice before asking for assistance. Allow extra time for underlining or highlighting key words and phrases.

239. Always check for understanding before the student begins the assignment.

240. For the visually impaired student, always give test directions, assignments, and other important instructions orally.

241. Place a piece of yellow acetate over the page of print to enhance the contrast for students with a visual impairment.

242. Use black felt-tip pens to trace over directions and darken large print for students with low vision.

Notes

"Doing something differently can make all the difference."
-Noah benShea

Chapter 16

Large Group Instruction

Oral Presentations

A large portion of a student's school day is spent listening to material presented orally. This may be in the form of a class lecture, a video, a movie, a speaker, or learning from peers. Classroom lectures are often difficult for students with special needs, especially for the student who experiences difficulty with auditory processing.

243. While listening to the lecture, write the goals and objectives of the lesson for the student. Discuss the goals and objectives with him before beginning the follow-up assignments.

244. Review previous lessons, notes, and vocabulary words with the student. Link new facts and materials to previously learned information.

245. When reviewing materials from a class lecture, present only the relevant information. Use nouns when possible. Leave out pronouns such as it, him, her, them, those, etc. The continual use of pronouns may cause confusion especially, if the student has not fully grasped the subject of the lecture.

246. Simplify the vocabulary when reviewing lecture notes with the student.

247. When presenting material orally, frequently ask the student to summarize the new information learned. Ask direct questions to check for understanding.

248. Be sure the student has removed all unnecessary materials from the desktop before the lecture begins. If the student is required to take notes during oral pres-

entations, two sharpened pencils, paper, and a highlighter should be the only objects on top of the desk.

Notetaking Skills

Notetaking is a difficult process. Think about the last time you attended a class or a workshop. Did you take notes on the syllabus provided? Perhaps you recorded the information to listen to in the car on the way home. Did you jot down key words and phrases? Or did you write entire phrases verbatim? Perhaps you were able to generalize the information and fill in a chart or a graph. When the presenter stated, "This is important!," did you furiously try to write every word? As adults, we use many strategies at different times and in different situations. Notetaking is not a simple skill. It requires the student to process information both auditorily and visually. The student must then output the information in a written format. Students must be taught various strategies to take notes successfully.

The book *Winning the Study Game – Learning How to Succeed in School* (listed in Appendix B) is a comprehensive study skills program and includes a great deal of information for helping students with special needs learn to effectively take notes.

249.   Encourage the student to take notes in his own words.

250.   Teach common abbreviations for notetaking. See Form #34 in Appendix A for a list of common abbreviations. This may be used as a guide or may be reproduced for older students.

251.   Provide the student with an outline of the main topics before the material is presented in class. Provide ample space so the student may take notes directly on the outline sheet.

252.   Before the presentation, read the discussion questions (if available) to the student. This will help the student to focus on the most important information.

253.   Teach key phrases such as "please remember this," "this point is very important," or "write this down." General education teachers use these words frequently when making key points.

254.   When comparing or contrasting information, provide the student with a chart so the information may be filled in.

255.   Timelines will help students to document information if the information is presented in chronological order.

256.   Teach the student to jot down key words if there is not enough time to complete the thought. You can assist the student with the organization at a later time.

257.   If the student is unable to take notes, allow a peer to use carbon paper, or photocopy the supervising teacher's notes. You may also take notes for the stu-

dent. If supplemental notes are provided to the student, it is important that he continues to practice taking notes during the class session.

258. Demonstrate how to highlight the important information from the student's notes after the lecture.

259. When the general education teacher uses an overhead projector with transparencies, the student with low vision should look directly into the overhead projector while the transparency is projected onto the wall. Discuss this with the vision teacher.

260. An overhead projector will assist the student with a hearing impairment. It will allow the student to see the presentation and read the teacher's lips simultaneously. Make sure the student is seated in an appropriate location.

261. Tape-record or make a video of the presentation. Allow the student to take it home for review.

Notes

"There is no failure except in no longer trying."
-Elbert Hubbard

Chapter 17

Classroom Assessments

There are two ways that classroom assessments may be modified. The supervising teacher may modify the content of the assessment for individual students based on their IEPs or the student may need instructional modifications with the actual test. As a paraprofessional some of your responsibilities with assessment may include monitoring the student during assessment activity, reading the test aloud, recording the student's answers, or perhaps helping the student organize his thoughts and ideas. Often, students will require alternate forms of assessment due to difficulties with reading and written language. If the goal is to measure the student's knowledge of a curriculum area, it is important to test only the curriculum and not to penalize the student for the disability.

262. Test orally instead of requiring the student to write the answers on paper.

263. Allow the student to demonstrate the concept currently being tested. Allow the student to illustrate or create a final project demonstrating mastery.

264. Write the answers to the questions for the student. Be sure to record the answers verbatim.

265. Allow the student extra time to complete the test. Administer the test outside the classroom area if possible, in a place that is free of distracting stimuli.

When supervising tests, especially those which have time constraints, ask the student to complete the items in which they are confident in the answer first, and then return to the more difficult test items.

266.   Read all test directions orally. Check for understanding.

267.   Tape record the test and allow the students to record their answers verbally.

268.   Maintain a record of the pretests and posttests. These records will reflect effort and improvement. The scores should be given to the special education teacher.

269.   If a test contains multiple parts, be sure each section includes a set of directions. Point out the various test sections and be sure the student understands the individual instructions.

270.   Ask students to circle, underline, or highlight key words in the directions. You may also do this for the student before the test is received.

271.   Use recognition of facts rather than factual recall on tests. If you encounter trick questions on commercially made tests, point these out to the supervising teacher. The teacher can make a decision as to whether or not to delete the question.

272.   If the district requires the student to take standardized tests, ask if it is possible to order consumable tests. This will eliminate the need to transfer the response to a computer score sheet. If a computer scorecard must be used, have the student complete the test on paper and you can record the answers when the student finishes.

Types of Assessments

The following assessments are the most common paper/pencil tests used in the classroom environment.   Some of the common instructional modifications are listed for each of the tests.

273.   **Essay Tests**. Essay tests are often the most difficult type of test for students with special needs. The test involves reading and understanding the question, recollection of information, organizing the thoughts, and transferring the information to paper. The following will help the student with essay tests.

  •   First, be certain the student understands the test question. Ask the student to paraphrase the question to check for understanding.

  •   Be certain the student understands the following direction words which regularly appear in the directions for essay exams: *compare, contrast, explain, describe,* and *list*.

  •   Help the student to create a simple outline. This will help him to organize and sequence his thoughts before writing.

- If allowed, provide a list of the key vocabulary words which the student may need for the essay. If there are additional words the student would like you to list (for example, words that may be difficult for the student to spell), also list these.

- For the student who experiences difficulty with written language, you may be asked to write the test for the student. If so, be sure to record it verbatim.

274. **Fill-in-the-Blank.** For this type of test, a word bank is frequently provided. If not, ask if one may be created for the student. Before testing, ask the student to read each word in the word bank and to recall as much information as possible about the individual words. If a word bank is used during the assessment, the student should draw a light pencil mark through the response in case it needs to be changed at a later time.

275. **Matching.** If the matching list is long, check with the supervising teacher to see whether or not the list may be divided into groups of 5-8 questions. This must be done under the direction of the supervising teacher, as the answer selections are decreased, which automatically increases the odds of the student receiving a higher grade. With matching tests, often there are clues within the sentence structure of the test. Help the student become aware of this. For example, if the beginning part of the sentence in column A is very long the odds are the second part in column B may be one of the shorter answers. If the first part of the sentence ends with the word *an*, the second part of the sentence will begin with a word that has an initial vowel sound. Simple strategies such as these are often easily grasped by general education students, while the student with special needs may be so intent on trying to read the material that the obvious clues are often missed.

276. **Multiple-Choice.** When taking a multiple-choice test, the student should read through the entire test first and answer only the questions for which he definitely knows the answers. Once this step is complete, the student should read the questions a second time, answering the questions which are familiar. With the remainder of the questions, the student should narrow his choices by first eliminating all answers which make no sense. When this is complete, he will need to make an educated guess. On multiple-choice tests there are often questions within the context of the text which may provide answers. Students should, therefore, be encouraged to read the entire test very carefully.

277. **Short Answer.** Short answer tests are very similar to essay tests. First, be sure that the student understands the test question. Check for understanding of the direction words (compare, contrast, explain, describe, and list) before starting the test. If appropriate, supply the student with a list of vocabulary words applicable to the unit.

278. **Standardized Tests.** Many standardized tests rely heavily on the student's ability to read the material. If the student reads at a level which is several years below grade level, this will be a frustrating experience. There are strict guidelines for administering standardized tests; therefore, they cannot be modified. Another area of concern with standardized testing is that the response sheet is often computer scored and students frequently lose their place when filling in the corresponding circles. If the student must take the test, one option is to use a consumable test booklet, if available. If a consumable test booklet is used, the answers will need to be transferred to the computer score card when the test is complete.

Standardized testing will be addressed by the special education team. If the student is excused from participation in the standardized testing, this fact will be addressed in the Individual Education Plan. In place of the testing, use the time for review, reteaching of materials, or previewing upcoming lessons.

279. **True-False.** This type of test is often difficult for students, as the test questions frequently contain double negatives. If you encounter this type of question, ask the supervising teacher if some of the questions may be rewritten.

"Punish the incident and treat the problem."
-Anonymous

Chapter 18

Behavior Management

Personal behavior is hard to change. Take a moment to think about your own life. Are there things you would like to change but have not because it is too difficult? Have you procrastinated at starting a daily exercise program because it is just too hard to fit into your schedule or it seems like too much work? As an adult, you have control over whether or not you choose to make these personal changes. Students struggle with the same issues with personal change. Their behaviors, although not acceptable in the school setting, may be accepted in their home environment. The student has had a great deal of time to develop and practice ways to avoid difficult situations. For many students, however, the behaviors are learned, and learned behaviors can be changed with patience, persistence, and positive reinforcement.

Why do students misbehave? Frequently, misbehavior for students with special needs is a cover-up for lack of success in the school environment. By acting out, the student avoids the embarrassment of being perceived as "dumb." Students may act out with the intention of being removed from the classroom, therefore avoiding the assignment which they were unable to complete. Students may also develop an "I don't care" attitude to avoid the work which they are incapable of doing. Therefore, students who struggle, often have to make a choice between looking like a bad kid (which is often perceived by their peers as a "cool" kid) or looking dumb in front of their peers. For many, the choice is an easy one.

So, as professionals, what do we do? We try to help the student become capable and successful in the classroom environment by modifying and adapting the curriculum so the student can succeed. At times, we also try to control the negative behavior by threatening, removing privileges, and contacting parents. This may work for some students, but for many, the options soon are used up and there is nothing else left to try.

When working with students who misbehave, patience is essential. Being patient and calm decreases the possibility of reinforcing the student's negative behavior. Staying calm also decreases the chance that you may respond out of anger and frustration or perhaps say or do something that you will later regret. Persistence is necessary, as the student must learn that there are consistent consequences for their actions. The consequence which occurs for a specific behavior on Monday should be the same consequence that also occurs on Tuesday, Wednesday, Thursday, and Friday. If you are not persistent and the consequence is not consistent, the student may continually repeat the behavior to see if he is able to "get away with it."

It is also imperative to respond to the student positively. This may seem ironic when discussing misbehavior, but it is important to "catch" the student in appropriate, responsible situations. Some students act out for attention. For these students, you need to find situations when they are acting responsibly so that you may complement and provide positive feedback, and conversely, there are times when it may be appropriate to ignore the inappropriate behavior. These responses may result in a decrease in the negative behavior.

The behavior of some students is so severe that a specific behavior plan needs to be followed. Many of these students take medication to help control their behavior. The supervising teacher will explain how to implement supplemental behavior plans and what to do when a situation is out of control and backup support is needed. The individual behavior plan developed by the special education team overrides the following information presented in this section

As a paraprofessional, you will work with students who have behavior difficulties. Therefore, it is important to anticipate and discuss specific situations with the supervising teacher in advance. Some basic questions have been formulated on Form #35 – "What do I do…" located in Appendix A.

Behavior Strategy Tips

280.   View misbehavior as a teachable moment. After an incident has occurred and the student has calmed down, discuss the behavior with the student and determine alternate forms of release. Form #36 – Behavior Change Plan may be filled out in conjunction with the student – or the student may fill it out alone. In place of the form, the student may answer the following questions on paper. The form should be given to the supervising teacher for follow-up.

- What happened?
- What happened before the incident?
- What was your response?
- How could you respond differently if the situation reoccurs?
- How can I help you? What do you need?

Form #36 – Sample Behavior Change Plan

What happened? (list the incident that occurred)	What happened before the incident? (list the activity, subject, or any helpful information)	How did I respond?	What are some alternate responses if this situation reoccurs?
I was kicked out of class.	Nothing. I was trying to do my work. John kept turning around and bugging me.	I threw my pencil at him and told him to shut his mouth.	I could try to ignore him. I suppose I could go sit someplace else.

Additional support or comments.

Talk to the classroom teacher and ask if there is an alternative place to sit if I can't get my work done in my assigned seat.

281.   Avoid power struggles with students. You will not gain anything.

282.   When dealing with difficult students, remain calm and speak in quiet, calm voice. Be aware of your personal body language.

283.   Don't get backed into a corner by making empty threats or threats that you are not prepared to follow through on. You will lose credibility quickly.

284.   Don't give in to anger. If you feel you are losing control, it may be best to walk away. Often the student wants your attention, and removing yourself from the situation no longer gives the student an audience.

285.   Do not take student comments personally. When a student acts out, you may be accused of being unfair and unreasonable. Keep in mind that these comments would be directed to any person of authority.

286.   Take time to think before responding. Count to ten, take several deep breaths, and think about your response before actually saying it. After pausing to think, you may decide that the best response is no response at all.

287.   Select your battles carefully. Some of the small battles are just not worth it. Ask your supervising teacher which issues are the most important and which ones can perhaps be overlooked.

288. Offer acceptable choices to the student. Think through the choices first as you will need to live with them. If in doubt, explain to the student that you need some time to think and then discuss the issue with the supervising teacher.

289. Ignore the student. Often the student has determined exactly what will "push your buttons." If this is the case, try to ignore the student as long as the action is not harmful or hurtful to others.

290. Proximity control is often used in the classroom. Stand or sit close to the student.

291. Some students do not realize that their habits are annoying to others. These habits may include continually blurting out answers, tapping a pencil on the desk, fidgeting with small items, etc. Create a visual signal to let the student know it is occurring and should stop.

292. Often, taking a short walk in the hall is enough to calm the student and avoid a possible explosive situation.

293. Humor can often defuse a situation. However, if you are not by nature a funny person, do not try to experiment with humor during a crisis situation. More than likely, the student will take it as sarcasm, since it is out of character.

294. Some students have a very low frustration level and tend to lash out when frustrated. If you notice that a student is becoming extremely frustrated with an assignment or activity, take a break and try it at a later time.

295. Often, students can sense when their behaviors are escalating to a point of no return. If the student is aware that an outburst is about to occur, he may need some time away from the classroom. Arrange a location free of stimulus where the student may go. This may be a counselor's office, the library, or any suitable quiet area in the classroom environment. This option should be listed in the IEP.

296. There may be times when a student is unable to calm down and refuses to leave the setting. If this happens, you may have to remove the other students from the situation and call for back-up support. If the situation is potentially dangerous, be sure to remove from the area all objects which the student could use to harm himself or others.

297. Don't expect changes to occur overnight. For some chronic misbehavior, you may have to correct, correct, and correct again. Change takes time. You may wonder how many times it will take to correct the behavior. The only answer is "as long as it takes."

298. As a paraprofessional, you may be asked to gather and document information in the classroom. The supervising teacher may ask you to "target" specific behaviors. A target behavior is a behavior that can be seen, is measurable and is well-

defined. Some examples of target behaviors may include ability to follow the teacher's direction within ten seconds, not arguing, following classroom rules, being on-task 80% of the time, being on time to class, etc.

At times when attention is focused on a target behavior for the student with special needs, it can easily be overlooked that the same behavior actually occurs frequently with students in the general population. A simple way to compare a target behavior of a specific student to the behavior of his peers is to use a tally sheet. To tally information, you will need to have a watch with a second hand and a tally sheet. Form #37 located in Appendix A is a reproducible tally sheet. On the tally sheet, student #1 is the target student. Select two or three other students in the classroom for comparison. For this hypothetical example, every 30 seconds you will glance at one of the students (student #1, #2, #3, in consecutive order) and make a mark if the student is on task. At the end of the observation time, you will have a good indicator of the student's on-task behavior in relation to his peers. The tally sheet may also be used to document behavior for the individual student.

Form #37 – Sample Tally Sheet

Student	Date / Time	Observable Behavior	
	March 10 9:00-9:15 am	On-task behavior during independent work time 30 second intervals	
		Tally Space	
#1 Target Student			**Total**
Peer #2			**Total**
Peer # 3			**Total**

Another option is to videotape the entire class and tally the target behaviors while viewing the video. With the video, it is easy to assess and document more than one target behavior at a time. The video is confidential information and should be erased once the observation is complete. The purpose of the tape is only for observation purposes.

299.   Consistency is important. Do not be lenient and easygoing on days when you feel good and then harsh on days when you feel tired or stressed.

300.   If you would like the student to do something, use statements and not questions. For example, if it is time for the student to clear off his desk tell him, "Please put

your things away now." Do not ask, "Would you like to put away your things?" You may not like the reply.

301.   Before giving a direction, be sure to have the student's attention. Look for eye contact. Give only one or two directions at a time.

Reinforcement and Discipline

302.   If the student consistently needs to be disciplined during a specific academic class, it is important to determine whether or not the current modifications are appropriate. Report this to the supervising teacher. Do not wait until the situation escalates.

303.   If a student disrupts the class frequently, report the behavior to the special education teacher. No student should be allowed to continually interfere with the education of the other students. An alternative for the student who repeatedly disrupts the class is to videotape the class presentation. The student can watch the video during the next class session and complete the assignment alone or with you. The student returns to the class when the assignment or lesson is complete. In this way, the student is still held responsible for the assignment. For many students who act out, the positive reinforcement received comes from the other students. When the student is removed the classroom, the audience is no longer available.

304.   At times, a student needs a place to get away from stimuli and regroup. Find a quiet place for the student. This may be in the classroom, in another classroom, or in a vacant area. Give the student a special pass to be used in this situation. If the area is in another classroom, a telephone code may be worked out with the cooperating teacher. One ring means the student is on the way. If the student does not arrive, the cooperating teacher can call back. The student may take classwork and complete it in this area. Rules must be set. An example of the rules may include:

- The work area may be used only during classwork times.
- A pass must be obtained from the classroom teacher when leaving the classroom area.
- You must return within a specified number of minutes.

305.   Often, students with behavior disorders are more dependent on external reinforcement than others in their peer group. In an inclusive setting, students may need constant reassurance that they are doing well. A reward system may help to meet this need in the classroom. Reward systems are also used frequently in the cafeteria, during study periods, or at recess.

Reward systems must be implemented cautiously. The purpose of a reward system is to help the student improve behavior. The good behavior and positive feedback that a student receives for behaving appropriately should be the final reward. As a result the final outcome of all reward systems is to eventually eliminate the tangible reward.

Therefore, when a reward system is used, the main focus is the positive verbal feedback and the tangible reward should be secondary. For this reason, positive comments should be emphasized with the student before you actually give the reward or point. Let's look at an example. Jerry's goal is to stay on task for increments of fifteen minutes. When Jerry meets this objective, an appropriate comment would be, "Jerry, you certainly have been working hard; show me what you have finished." Once you have checked and commented on the assignment, the point may be applied.

306. There are many types of reward systems. Before deciding on the type of system to use, you need to establish a list of reinforcement activities or rewards for the student. It is important to establish the list with the student. Some examples of rewards may include extra computer time, time to chat with friends, choosing a friend for a special activity, omission of a homework assignment (at the teacher's discretion), or something as simple as being the first student in line. Be sure the list of reinforcements is approved by the supervising teacher before beginning.

Once the reinforcement has been approved, the supervising teacher will help determine how the day should be divided and how the reward system will be implemented. If the target behavior for the student is to stay on task during independent worktime, feedback may be required every five to ten minutes. If the target behavior is to complete and return daily assignments, a chart may be used only during the morning check-in. The supervising teacher will provide clear guidelines as to when and why the points will be awarded.

307. Charts may be used to record the student's behavior. As you walk around the class place a check mark or a sticker onto the chart for appropriate behavior and work completion. When the card is full, it may be turned in for a reward. Some reinforcement charts are included on Form #38 in Appendix A. The charts are very generic and may be adapted to meet the student's individual needs. For younger students, cute and colorful charts with matching stickers may be purchased from teacher supply stores.

For older students, a simple positive reinforcement phrase or a pat on the back often is sufficient reinforcement.

308. Keep parents informed when the student has shown improvement during the day. Create a list of positive sayings such as the following:

Awesome Day!
I discovered the secret to success today!
Super Star!
I'm a Great Student!
Wow!

Photocopy the sayings from Form #39 in Appendix A onto fluorescent paper or onto an 8 ½" x 11" full label sheet so students may stick it on their notebooks or folders. Cut the phrases apart and place them into an envelope. When the student has a good day, a phrase strip is selected to take home. If proper guidelines are set, older students will be able to monitor their own progress. Rewards may be given when the student has received a specific number of positive phrases. This is a simple way to communicate with the parents. Some parents may also offer an incentive in the home.

309. A point system may be implemented. Points may be assigned to each class block and frequently range from from zero to three. The supervising teacher will determine the guidelines for receiving the points. Homework assignments may also be included on the sheet. A space for positive comments should be included on the chart. At the end of the week, points are tallied and the student receives a predetermined reward if the individual goal has been met. This is appropriate for older students. Form #40 in Appendix A includes a sample worksheet which may be reproduced.

310. A token system works well for many students. The tokens may consist of small laminated paper shapes, buttons, beads, or whatever else might be easy to keep in your possession. Tokens may be distributed randomly to the student for appropriate behavior. The student keeps the tokens in a container, and when the student has the predetermined number of tokens, they may be exchanged for rewards. If the "cost" of the rewards varies, encourage students to set long-term goals and save their tokens until a goal is achieved.

Tokens may also be used in the reverse. The student receives a set number of tokens upon arrival in the morning. He returns a token every time an inappropriate behavior occurs. At the end of the day, the student may use the remainder of the tokens for a reward. When using this method, be sure that the student clearly understands the rules before beginning. The rules should be specific and in writing. A rule such as "respect others" is hard to enforce. Therefore, it is better to write a rule such as "Do not talk when others are talking," "Wait until you are called on before answering," and "Do not take other people's belongings." These rules are clear and concise.

311.   The class discipline plan may not be appropriate for all students. Students may need a supplemental discipline plan with extra warnings, coupled with a reward system. Some students should only receive one warning, or they tend to take advantage of the system. Other students may need several. The supervising teacher will provide the supplemental discipline plan. All adults involved should be aware of the plan and follow it.

312.   A daily report can be used to monitor behavior and academic goals. An easy way to create a daily report is to tape an index card to the student's desk. Subjects are added to the card throughout the day. For younger students, a happy face may be placed on the card after the subject if the student has experienced success during the time block. For older students, a rating scale of zero to three may be used. Form #41 in Appendix A may be used for older students. This report may be sent home daily to increase communication between the school and the home.

313.   A daily log has proven successful in coordinating home and school communication. The log is usually a spiral notebook that remains in the backpack daily. Both parents and teachers use this log to write comments, concerns, and suggestions. The student is rewarded for taking home and returning the notebook daily.

314.   Teach the student to use positive self-talk. "I can do this!" "I can handle this!" or "I'm good at this!" are all examples of self-talk. If you hear a student using negative self-talk or putting himself down, stop him and help him to rephrase the comments positively.

ADD/ADHD

Some students with disabilities are also medically diagnosed as ADD (Attention Deficit Disorder) or ADHD (Attention Deficit Hyperactivity Disorder). Modifications need to be made within the classroom setting if the student is to experience success in school. For the majority of these students, the strategies and modifications discussed previously in this book will be helpful in the classroom. The strategies in this section pertain directly to the student who experiences difficulty with attention, on-task behavior, impulsivity, or distractibility.

Not all students with a medical diagnosis of ADD receive service under the umbrella of special education. In order to receive service, the student must have a primary handicapping condition that meets the Federal guidelines for special education. Students who do not meet this criterion may receive additional support in the classroom under a 504 Plan. If this is the case, the supervising teacher is the general education teacher and the special education department is not directly involved with the service for the student. At this time, the topic of ADD is being discussed at the Federal level and perhaps, someday, these students will also receive service under the umbrella of special education.

Providing Structure

315.   Daily structure needs to be provided for all students, but for these students it is especially important. Transition times are difficult and should be closely monitored. If the general education teacher does not have a daily schedule posted, create one for the student. Discuss the schedule and point out daily changes in advance.

316.   Provide a visual cue to the student several minutes before a transition is to occur. The student may need extra time to adjust and organize materials before beginning a new subject. Provide extra structure during transition times. Many students tend to get into trouble during transition times; therefore, monitor these times closely.

317.   Review the classroom rules frequently. If a student is having difficulty with a specific rule, write down the rule. Be clear and concise. A student cannot argue with a piece of paper. Give specific examples of the rule. Examples may include sitting quietly while the teacher is talking, staying in your seat when the teacher is talking, or sharpening pencils at the beginning of the class period.

318.   Always state the positive action you would like to see. For example, if the student is running in the hall, simply say, "Walk, please."

319.   Check-in and check-out times are important for the student. Go to the student's classroom. Use this time to check homework and assignment books or to remind the student to turn in completed projects and assignments.

Working with the Student

320.   Make sure you have the student's attention when talking to him. You may have to ask him to physically stop the current activity to get his attention.

321.   Include the student in small group activities and instruction whenever possible. Immediate feedback is important.

322.   Provide one- or two-step directions only. Ask the student to repeat directions back to you. Check for understanding of each direction.

323.   Give one assignment at a time. Many students with ADD are overwhelmed easily. Keep all assignments in a folder. If the student falls behind, complete some of the assignments orally to catch up.

324.   Allow ample time for hands-on instruction. This will help actively engage the student in the learning process. Active participation is extremely important for this student. It will assist him in remaining focused.

325. Modify daily assignments to alleviate frustration. (See the section on Daily Assignments.)

326. Use computer instruction for academic reinforcement when appropriate. The computer provides immediate feedback, self-paced instruction, and increased motivation.

327. Use a timer to assist students with on-task behavior. Explain the task you would like the student to complete and then set the timer for the specified amount of time. Start with a short assignment so the student is successful. Longer assignments may be divided into sections. Once the student is able to stay on task for the specified amount of time, increase the time by one or two minutes.

328. Allow the student time during the day to get up, walk around, and stretch. It may be appropriate for the student to sit in the back of the classroom so he is able to stand or sit as needed with minimal disruption to the class. If movement is necessary, provide clear guidelines about when movement is appropriate.

329. Many students benefit from immediate feedback. Provide self-correctors so the student is able to correct his own assignments as they are complete. For example, once the student has completed five math problems, allow him to correct the problems before proceeding to the next group.

330. Often ADD students have difficulty making decisions. When appropriate allow the student to choose between two or among three activities. In this manner, tasks are still completed, but the student is allowed a small amount of control.

Impulsivity and Distractibility

331. Seat the student in a location with limited visual stimuli. Artwork or cluttered walls may distract the student from lessons.

332. Check seating arrangements. Students should not be seated near doors, windows, or high traffic areas.

333. Allow extra time to complete assignments, even if the assignments have been modified.

334. Timed activities and tests should be avoided. Many students become frustrated when they notice that others have completed an assignment and then tend to guess or give up. Discuss alternate activities with the supervising teacher.

335. Teach the student to stop and think before responding. Create a visual signal between you and the student. An example of a visual signal would be to place your finger aside your nose. When the student observes this, he will know that it is time to slow down and think about the action.

336.   Use visual clues for movement. A simple technique is to place one red and one green cup within the student's sight. Stack the cups. When the red cup is on top, the student must remain seated. When the green cup is placed on top the student may move about the classroom. This can also be done using red and green construction paper.

337.   Teach students to talk to themselves. Often, students are heard using negative self-talk. Try to reverse this to positive self-talk. The student may say to himself, "I can do this" over and over. For some students, repeating the directions out loud is especially helpful when complex steps and directions are given. It will also assist the student in remaining focused on the current task.

338.   If possible, the student should be seated near quiet, independent workers who are good role models. Do not seat disruptive or easily distracted students together.

339.   Allow the student to have only the necessary materials for the current assignment on top of the desk. Toys and play objects should remain at home. If the student must have something in hand, give him a small piece of clay, a small balloon filled with flour, or a stress ball to squeeze.

A Final Note from the Author

The paraprofessional's job is essential to every inclusive setting. In school districts nationwide, the number of paraprofessionals is equal to or exceeds the number of special education teachers employed. Whether you are employed several hours per week or as a fulltime employee, you are a vital part of the program. Inclusive settings cannot exist without your support.

Not everyone can be a paraprofessional. The job is very demanding. You may be required to work with many students and teachers throughout the day. This requires extreme flexibility on your part. Communication skills are important; a positive attitude, enthusiasm, and patience are also crucial for success.

Though the job is demanding, the rewards are numerous! The rewards might include the dazzling smile of a student who has just learned to read, the sparkle of success in the eyes of a child unable to communicate verbally, the encouragement of classmates when a student is faced with a difficult challenge, or the feeling you have of knowing that you make a positive difference in the lives of many children. Without your support, inclusive settings would cease to exist.

Whether you are thinking about applying for a job, have been recently hired, or are an experienced paraprofessional, I hope this book will provide you with the support you need.

Write to me at Peytral Publications and tell me about your experiences. If you have specific comments, suggestions, or questions that have not been addressed in this book, let me know.

I wish you good luck. You will make a difference in the lives of many.

Peggy Hammeken

Ω

Notes

Appendix A

Form #1

Contact List

Name and Position	Contact Information	Notes

Form #2, page 1

Discussion Activities for Paraprofessionals

The general education teacher asks you to go to the office and pull the confidential files for some of the students in her math class. You do not work with these students.

In the classroom you overhear a group of students making negative comments about one of the students you support in the classroom.

The classroom teacher asks you to contact the parents about discipline problems that have occurred during the day.

The supervising general education teacher consistently leaves the classroom, leaving you in charge of all the students.

Form #2, page 2

Discussion Activities for Paraprofessionals

You feel that your supervising general education teacher treats several students in an unprofessional manner. You do not want to approach him so you decide to discuss the situation with some of your colleagues.

Your own child has just been diagnosed with ADD. You know that several students with Learning Disabilities also are diagnosed as ADD. You want to find out the types of medication and the dosage that these students take. You decide to talk to the nurse about these children.

You attend a party at a friend's house and discover that the parents of a student you support are also at the party. The parents start asking you about their child's progress. Later, your friend asks you for specifics about the child.

As a paraprofessional, part of your job description includes helping a student who uses a wheelchair to get through the lunch line and situated at the table. While the student is eating, you monitor the lunchroom and chat with students. While roving throughout the lunchroom, you hear a group of girls discussing someone who has been sexually assaulted.

Form #3

General Responsibilities

Paraprofessional Responsibility	Training Needed	Follow-Up Date

Form #4

Roles and Responsibilities

Educator Activity	Paraprofessional Activity	Date

Form #5

Daily Schedule

Time	Location	Activity	Supervising Teacher

Form #6

Daily Log

Student:_____ **Date:**_____ M T W TH F

Student:_____ **Date:**_____ M T W TH F

Student:_____ **Date:**_____ M T W TH F

Student:_____ **Date:**_____ M T W TH F

Student:_____ **Date:**_____ M T W TH F

Form #7

Daily Communication

Student's Name:_____ Date:_____

Daily notes or comments:_____

_____

_____

_____

_____

_____

_____

☐   See me regarding this
☐   Speak to the classroom teacher
☐   Call the parent
☐   _____

Daily Communication

Student's Name:_____ Date:_____

Daily notes or comments:_____

_____

_____

_____

_____

_____

_____

☐   See me regarding this
☐   Speak to the classroom teacher
☐   Call the parent
☐   _____

Form #8

Back-Up Discipline Plan

Student's Name: _____ Date: _____

Special Education Contact: _____
General Education Contact: _____

Back-Up Discipline Plan:

_____
_____
_____
_____
_____

Additional Information:

_____
_____
_____
_____
_____
_____

If assistance is needed please call the following person(s).

Contact Person with Telephone Number

❑   Administrator   _____
❑   General Education   _____
❑   Special Education   _____
❑   Paraprofessional   _____
❑   Parent   _____
❑   _____   _____
❑   _____   _____
❑   _____   _____

Form #9

Medical Alert Form

Student's Name: _____

General Education Contact: _____

❑ **This is an emergency situation. Call 911 immediately and then contact the following people.**

Contact Person and Telephone Number
1. _____
2. _____
3. _____

Notes: _____
_____
_____
_____

Area of Concern: _____
_____
_____
_____

Symptoms: _____
_____
_____
_____

Additional Information: _____
_____
_____
_____
_____
_____
_____

Copies:
❑ General Education   ❑ _____
❑ Special Education   ❑ _____
❑ Nurse   ❑ _____
❑ Paraprofessional   ❑ _____
❑ Parent

Form #10, page 1

General Classroom Information

Classroom Teacher: _____   Subject Area: _____

Student List:

_____

_____

_____

Classroom Schedule: (What is my daily schedule? When will student contact occur? Planning time?)

Classroom Instruction: (How will I help students in the classroom? Where and when will I receive training? What are your expectations? Will I be involved with student planning?)

Form #10, page 2

General Classroom Information

Student Evaluation: (Will I have a role in student evaluation? Will I be expected to document and monitor student progress? If yes, who will provide training and guidance?)

Classroom Rules: (What are the classroom rules? Are all students expected to follow the same rules or are there exceptions?)

Consequences: (Who is responsible for implementing the consequences if a student does not follow the rules? Are the consequences the same for all students? Are there rewards as well as consequences?)

Communication: (When will we find time to communicate our needs? Will I be expected to communicate with parents? When will we find time to communicate as a team? Who is my primary contact person?)

Use the back of this form to list additional information which is relevant to this classroom.

Form #11

Goal Worksheet

Student: _____ Subject Area: _____

General Education Teacher: _____

Special Education Teacher: _____

Date:
Final Goal:
Short Term Objectives:

Date:
Final Goal:
Short Term Objectives:

Date:
Final Goal:
Short Term Objectives:

Form #12

Instructional Changes

Date: _____

Student: _____

Subject Area: _____

Area of Difficulty	Instructional Modification Implemented	Result

Curriculum Modifications

Date:_____
Student's Name:_____
Team Members: _____
_____
_____
_____

List the student's strengths:

List the student's goals:

MODIFICATIONS

Textbook:

Person responsible for follow-up:

Daily Assignments:

Person responsible for follow-up:

Spelling:

Person responsible for follow-up:

Form #13, page 2

Curriculum Modifications

Mathematics:
Person responsible for follow-up:
Organizational Skills
Person responsible for follow-up:
Directions:
Person responsible for follow-up:
Large Group Instruction:
Person responsible for follow-up:
Assessment:
Person responsible for follow-up:
Behavior:
Person responsible for follow-up:
Additional Areas of Concern: (Use the back side of this form.)

Form #14, page 1

Textbook Modifications

Student's Name_____ Date: _____

Subject Area: _____ Grade level: _____

Team Members:

Check all that apply:

❏ The student will need modifications to the classroom textbook.
❏ The student should read the textbook with a peer or in a small group.
❏ The textbook should be provided on audiocassette.
  ❏ Full text version
  ❏ Paraphrase
  ❏ Alternate format _____
❏ Other:_____
❏ Other:_____
❏ Other:_____

❏ Name of person responsible:_____

Check all that apply:

❏ The student will need the following supplemental services:
  ❏ Preteaching and previewing of the material
  ❏ Outline of required units
  ❏ List of vocabulary words
  ❏ Checklist of required assignments and due dates
  ❏ Study guide
  ❏ Set of textbooks for home use
❏ Other:_____
❏ Other:_____
❏ Other:_____

❏ Person responsible for creating the modification:_____

Form #14, page 2

Textbook Modifications

Check all that apply:

❏ The student will require direct support from the Special Education Department.
    ❏ Supplemental curriculum is needed.
    ❏ _____
    ❏ _____
    ❏ _____
    ❏ _____

❏ List the person who will provide the direct instruction with the supplemental text-book.
    ❏ Direct instruction to be provided by:_____
    ❏ Location of direct service:_____
    ❏ Time of day:_____

❏ Support needed in the classroom
    ❏ _____
    ❏ _____
    ❏ _____
    ❏ _____

❏ Name of person responsible:_____

❏ Additional information

Form #15, page 1

Daily Assignment Modification Checklist

Student's Name_____ **Date:** _____

Subject Area: _____ **Grade Level:** _____

Team Members:

Check all that apply:

❒ The student will need the following applied to daily assignments:
  ❒ Modify the length of the assignment
  ❒ Place the student in cooperative groups whenever possible
  ❒ Allow the student to complete assignments orally
  ❒ Allow material to be read to the student
  ❒ Allow assignments to be written for the student
  ❒ Allow the student extra time to complete assignments
  ❒ The student is required to keep an assignment book
  ❒ Other:_____
  ❒ Other:_____
  ❒ Other:_____
  ❒ Other:_____
  ❒ Other:_____

❒ Person responsible for creating the modification:_____

Check all that apply:

❒ The student will need the following supplemental material and service:
  ❒ A checklist of assignments and due dates
  ❒ Textbooks for home use
  ❒ Consumable textbooks
  ❒ Other:_____
  ❒ Other:_____
  ❒ Other:_____
  ❒ Other:_____
  ❒ Other:_____

❒ Person responsible for creating the modification:_____

Form #15, page 2

Daily Assignment Modification Checklist

Check all that apply:

❏ The student will require direct support from the Special Education Department.
    ❏ Amount of service provided daily _____
    Location and time of service: _____
    Person responsible _____

❏ Supplemental curriculum will be provided.
    ❏ Alternative curriculum will be provided by _____
    ❏ Parallel activities will be provided by_____
    ❏ Other:_____
    ❏ Other:_____
    ❏ Other:_____

❏ Person responsible for student's program:_____

❏ Additional information:

Form #16

Assessment Checklist

Student's Name:_____ Date: _____
Subject Area: _____ Grade Level: _____

Team Members:

Check all that apply:

❏ The student will need the following applied to assessment situations:
    ❏ Allow extra or extended time
    ❏ Review materials with student prior to assessment
    ❏ Read the test aloud
    ❏ Student may respond to questions orally
    ❏ Student may use a vocabulary list during assessment
    ❏ Student may dictate or record the answers
    ❏ Assessment questions may be reworded and explained
    ❏ Student is allowed to use notes or study guide during assessment
    ❏ Student may use a calculator
    ❏ Student may use a computer
    ❏ Student may work with another student
    ❏ Other:_____
    ❏ Other:_____
    ❏ Other:_____
    ❏ Other:_____
    ❏ Other:_____
    ❏ Other:_____

❏ Additional comments:

❏ Person responsible for creating the modification:_____

Form #17

Volunteer List

Student Name	Dates				

Form #18

Daily Assignments

Date	Subject Area	Assignment	Due Date	Complete √

Form #19

Assignment Sheet

SUBJECT AREA	MONDAY	TUESDAY	WEDNESDAY	THURSDAY	FRIDAY
MATH					
SOCIAL STUDIES					
ENGLISH					
SCIENCE					
TESTS					
PROJECTS					

Sample Alphabet Activities

Letter	Activity
A	**Apple Art**. Cut an apple in half so that you can see the star. Dip the apple in paint and make apple prints. Have students cut out various colored apples from construction paper. Please "a" words on the apples and create an apple tree.
B	**Bean Art**. Provide the student several different kinds of dried beans. The student glues the beans to construction paper to make a design. Give each student a small brown bag. Ask the student to fill the bag with pictures of "b" words.
C	**Collage Art**. Help the student find pictures of things which begin with "c" in old magazines or select a subject such as cats, candy, colors, etc., and make a collage with the pictures. Fill a Campbell® Soup Can with words beginning with "c" words.
D	**Magic Door Art**. Cut four to six doors in piece of colored construction paper. Glue the construction paper on top of another piece of construction paper or tagboard. The student draws pictures of "d" words (duck, dog, doll, dandelion, dish and dinosaur) behind each door. Write a simple story about the items found behind the magic door.
E	**Egg Art**. Punch a small hole in one end of an egg and a larger hole in the other end. Blow out the contents and rinse the egg. The student can decorate the egg with markers or paints. Fill an envelope with "e" words.
F	**Fishbowl Art**. Students cut out small fish and write "f" words on them. Once the words are written, the students decorate the fish and glue them into a large fish bowl. Discuss fire prevention and fire drills with the student.
G	**Garden Art**. Students draw a garden with various flowers. The flowers may be decorated with glue and glitter. Create a grocery graph. Students cut out pictures from grocery ads and classify the items into groups on a piece of large construction paper.

Form #20, page 2

Sample Alphabet Activities

H	**Body Parts**. Trace the student's body on a large sheet of paper. Label the body parts that begin with h: hair, hands, heart, heel, head, and hips. What makes me happy? Create a list of happy thoughts.
I	**Insect Art**. Draw pictures of insects. Remember that insects have six legs, and their bodies are made up of the head, thorax, and abdomen. Label the body parts. Practice writing "i" sentences.
J	**Jewelry Art**. Have student's string macaroni and make a piece of jewelry. **Jelly Bean Sort.** Give each student a handful of jelly beans, and each student can sort the jelly beans by color.
K	**Kangaroo Art**. Provide a kite template for the student to cut out and decorate. Add colored ribbon or string. Draw pictures of "k" words and decorate the kites. **Random Acts of Kindness.** Discuss kindness with students, and ask each student to do some secret kind acts for friends and family.
L	**Leaf Art**. Provide an assortment of leaves and crayons or chalk. Make leaf rubbings on paper. Talk about what it means to be lazy, and write a group story about a lazy animal such as a lion, ladybug, lizard, or lamb.
M	**Macaroni or Mini Marshmallow Art.** Provide various shaped macaroni or colored mini marshmallows. The student decorates a large letter "m" by gluing the macaroni and marshmallows to the letter. Look around the room and discuss the various maps. Ask the students to make a map of their classroom.
N	**Nutrition Art**. Provide the student with a paper plate. The student cuts pictures of various healthy foods and glues the pictures onto the plate to create a nutritious meal. Visit the school nurse and have students ask questions about the nurse's job.

Form #20, page 3

Sample Alphabet Activities

O	**Opposite Art**. Discuss the concept of opposites, and have the student make a small book depicting such opposites as day/night, white/black, up/down, open/close, happy/sad, over/under, etc. Discuss the word "occupation" and talk about what the student would like to do as an adult.
P	**Pipe Cleaner Art**. Provide the student with several different colored pipe cleaners, and have the students make sculptures. Take turns placing small objects into your pocket. Begin by saying "I have something in my pocket…" and describe the item. The student needs to guess what you are hiding.
Q	**Q-tip® Art.** Give the student three or four small Q-tip® swaps. Dip them in paint and create a picture. Discuss the word "quiet." What does quiet mean? When is it important to be quiet and why?
R	**Rock Art.** Paint a rock to use as a paperweight. Discuss the importance of recycling. Have the student label paper bags and sort the various papers (plain, glossy, newsprint) for recycling.
S	**Sponge-Painting Art.** Cut a large sponge into small squares. The student dips the sponge into the paint and creates a design on white construction paper. Discuss the word "share." The student may also bring something from home to share.
T	**Tear Art.** Have the students create a picture by tearing small pieces of leftover paper and gluing the pieces to make a picture or a design. Discuss the five senses placing the emphasis of taste and touch. For taste, bring samples of various spices from home for the student to taste (a small pinch of sugar, salt, cinnamon, etc.) For touch, enclose small objects in a paper bag and ask the student to guess what the object is without looking.

Sample Alphabet Activities

U	**Undersea Art.** Using crayons on white construction paper, have the student draw pictures of undersea animals. When finished, dilute blue tempera paint with water and paint over the entire picture.
	Discuss the words "under" and "upside-down." List as many objects as possible in the classrooms that are under something. Determine the effect when some objects are upside-down. For example, what would happen if the waste basket, an open jar of paint, etc., were turned upside down?
V	**Vacation Art.** Students draw a picture of a previous vacation or a dream vacation to share.
	Discuss types of vacations and various transportation options: car, airplane, boat and train.
W	**Web Art.** Students use white chalk and black paper to draw interesting spider web designs. Create a small white spider and dangle it from the web on a white string.
	Take a walk to the nurse's office and weigh the student. If there is a science scale in the classroom, students may want to practice weighing various classroom objects.
X	**Cross-stitch Art**. Students use graph paper to make a design filled in by Xs.
	Discuss the use of X-rays with students. (broken bones, airport screening, etc) Find pictures of X-ray results to share with students.
Y	**Yarn Art.** Provide the student with yellow yarn in various lengths. The student places thin lines of glue on a piece of yellow construction paper and secures the yarn to the glue. Students may also use yellow glitter and fabric to complete their design.
	Discuss the reason for signal lights with special emphasis on the "caution" (yellow) light.
Z	**Zoo Art.** Have students create an imaginary animal on white construction paper. Cut strips of colored paper and glue these onto the paper to make a cage. Name the animal with a "z" name.
	Provide zip lock bags to students and have each student put "z" words into the bag.

Some of these ideas were adapted from the book <u>Hands-On-Phonics for Elementary Children</u> which is an excellent resource for beginning readers. It is listed in the Resource Section in Appendix B.

Story Starters

Titles

The Day I Missed My Own Party	The Rescue
The African Safari	If My Dog (Cat, Horse...) Could Talk
The Day I Made the News	The Mysterious Key
The Time Machine	I Really Saw an Alien!
The Grand Slam	The Day the Sun did not Set
The Tornado (Hurricane, Earthquake)	9-1-1
The Fire	Lost in the Forest (Jungle, Cave)
Help! I'm Invisible! (Shrinking, Growing)	The Substitute Teacher
If I were the Principal (President, Teacher)	My Secret Powers
If I were an Octopus (Barracuda, Shark)	HELP!
A Horrible (Wonderful, Depressing) Day	The Best Vacation Ever!

Beginning Sentences

I was sinking deeper and deeper into the quicksand...

I heard a loud growl directly behind me...

As the airplane reached full altitude, I sat back and closed my eyes. Finally...

I must be dreaming. I sat up and looked around. Everything was different...

Susan heard a scream. She ran to the lake to find her little brother...

I looked at the small snake in the box. My parents will never find out...

I slammed on the brakes. "Please stop!" I prayed...

Form #21, page 2

Story Starters

Beginning Sentences (continued)

I tried to run but the wind was so strong…

I hit the snooze button on the alarm for the third time. I just cannot go to school today…

I heard the rustle of the leaves. Slowly I walked toward the sound. Imagine my surprise when I found…

I picked up the wallet from the ground and opened it. The wallet had over $1000 dollars in cash…

Unbelievable Excuses

I don't have my homework because…

I ate the entire gallon of ice cream because…

I had to have my cell phone in class because.

I missed volleyball practice because…

I couldn't clean my bedroom because…

I didn't study for the test because…

I pretended to be sick because…

I gave the dog a haircut because…

I sneaked out the window at 2:00 am because…

I was late because…

I didn't go to school because…

I lied because…

I put worms in the sink because…

I had to skip class because…

I had to go to the movie because…

I dyed my hair green because…

I had to skip class because…

I missed the bus because…

Story Planner

Title: _____

Setting: _____

Season: _____

Time of Day: _____

Main Characters (include description also):

Character #1: _____

_____

_____

_____

Character #2: _____

_____

_____

_____

Character #3: _____

_____

_____

_____

_____

_____

Story Planner

How does the story begin? _____

_____

List the major events which occur in the story:

Event #1 _____

_____

_____

_____

Event #2 _____

_____

_____

_____

Event #3` _____

_____

_____

How does the story end? _____

_____

_____

_____

Form #23, page 1

Story Outline

1. Who is the main character in the story?

_____

_____

_____

2. List the other characters in the story:_____

_____

_____

_____

_____

3. What does the main character want to do (accomplish, solve) in the story?_____

_____

_____

_____

4. List the main events in the order in which they occur:

Event #1:_____

_____

_____

_____

Event #2:_____

_____

_____

_____

Event #3:_____

_____

_____

_____

Form #23, page 2

Story Outline

5. What happens as a result of the actions or the events? _____

_____

_____

_____

_____

_____

6. How does the story end? _____

_____

_____

_____

_____

List additional information you would like to include here:

_____

_____

_____

_____

_____

_____

_____

_____

_____

_____

_____

_____

_____

_____

_____

Form #24

Proofreading Checklists

Capital Letters	☐ **beginning of sentences** ☐ **names** ☐ **specific places** ☐ **title of story**
Punctuation	☐ **.** ☐ **?** ☐ **!**
Spelling	☐ **dictionary** ☐ **notes**

☐ Spelling
 	
 ☐ Punctuation
 	
 ☐ Capital Letters
 	
 ☐ Paragraphs
    ☐ indented
    ☐ topic sentence
    ☐ details
 	
 ☐ Margins
 	
 ☐ Overall Appearance
 	
 ☐ Name, Date, Class Period
	☐ Spelling
	
	 ☐ Punctuation
	
	 ☐ Appearance
	
	 ☐ Capitalization
	
	 ☐ Error Analysis

Form #25, page 1

Paragraph Sequencing Sample Activity

Each paragraph below contains mixed-up sentences. Read the sentences carefully. When you finish, cut the sentences apart and put them in the correct order so the paragraph makes sense.

Sample Paragraph

Mary then gathered the supplies needed to mix the cake.

She took the box of cake mix out of the cupboard and read the directions.

Thirty minutes later the timer went off and the cake was finished.

Once the batter was mixed she poured it into the pan and put the pan in the oven.

Mary decided to bake a cake for her mother's birthday.

Sample Paragraph

He knew he had to clean it, but did not know where to begin.

Once it was picked up and put away, John decided to vacuum.

John's bedroom was a mess.

He decided first to pick up all the stuff on the floor.

After several hours the job was finally complete.

Paragraph Sequencing Sample Activity

Sample Paragraph

Alisa knew she had to hurry or she would miss the school bus.

She grabbed her coat and mittens from the front closet.

She quickly put on her coat and zipped it up.

Next she put on her mittens.

She grabbed her backpack and rushed out the door to catch the bus.

Sample Paragraph

As he was mentally preparing to jump into the pool, the fire alarm sounded.

"I really don't feel like swimming 50 laps today," he thought as he entered the pool area.

"Yes! Saved by the alarm," he shouted as he grabbed his warm-ups and headed for the exit.

He then walked over to the pool to test the water.

It felt cold as ice and John shivered at the thought of jumping in.

He removed his warm-ups and threw them onto the bench.

John was in a terrible mood as he left the men's locker room.

Form #25, page 3

Paragraph Sequencing Activity

Name: _____

Date: _____

_____
Title

Form #26

Common Word Families

Beginning Word Families		More Advanced Word Families	
-am	am, ham, jam, Pam,	**-all**	ball, hall, mall, tall
-an	an, can, fan, man	**-ame**	blame, came, fame, game
-ap	cap, gap, lap, map	**-ank**	bank, rank, sank, tank
-at	at, cat, fat, hat	**-ash**	cash, flash, rash, trash
-ay	day, gay, hay, say	**-ate**	date, fate, mate, plate,
-ed	bed, fed, led, red	**-eat**	beat, feat, heat, treat
-ew	dew, few, new, pew	**-eed**	deed, feed, heed, seed
		-est	best, nest, pest, test
-in	fin, win, pin, chin		
-ip	dip, hip, lip, flip	**-ice**	dice, mice, nice, price
-it	it, bit, fit, sit	**-ick**	kick, lick, sick, brick
		-ide	hide, ride, pride, tide
-op	hop, mop, pop, crop	**-ight**	light, night, right, sight
-ot	dot, got, lot, plot	**-ill**	fill, hill, pill, will
-ow	bow, cow, how, now	**-ine**	fine, line, mine, vine
		-ink	link, pink, sink, wink
-ug	bug, dug, hug, rug		
-up	up, cup, pup,	**-ock**	dock, lock, clock, shock
-um	gum, drum, hum, plum	**-oke**	joke, choke, croak, poke
		-out	pout, scout, shout, trout
-ack	lack, tack, black, sack		
-ade	fade, made, blade, shade,	**-uck**	buck, puck, suck, stuck
-ail	bail, hail, nail, pail	**-ump**	bump clump, dump, lump

Form #27

Instant Words
This list of 100 words makes up almost one-half of all written material.

Words 1-25	Words 26-50	Words 51-75	Words 75-100
the	or	will	number
of	one	up	no
and	had	other	way
a	by	about	could
to	word	out	people
in	but	many	my
is	not	then	than
you	what	them	first
that	all	these	water
it	were	so	been
he	we	some	call
was	when	her	who
for	your	would	oil
on	can	make	its
are	said	like	now
as	there	him	find
with	use	into	long
his	an	time	down
they	each	has	day
I	which	look	did
at	she	two	get
be	do	more	come
this	how	write	made
have	their	go	may
from	if	see	part

Form #28

Common Prefixes and Suffixes

Prefix	Meaning	Sample Words
anti-	against	antiwar, antislavery
be-	make	befriend
bi-	two	bicycle, bifocals
circu-	around	circulate, circumference
contra-	against, opposite	contrary, contrast
dis-	not	disagree, disappear
ex-	former	ex-president, ex-student
hyper-	excessive	hyperactive, hypersensitive
in-	into	inside, infiltrate
inter-	among, between	intermission, interrupt
intra-	within	intravenous, intramural
mid-	middle	midway, midyear
mis-	wrong, not	mistake, misunderstand
multi-	many, much	multiply, multicolored
non-	not	nonfiction, nonstop
para-	almost	paramedic, paralegal
post-	after	postdate, postwar
pre-	before	pretest, prefix
pro-	favor	pro-war, pro-education
re-	again	remake, reread
sub-	under	subway, subzero
tele-	distant	telephone, telescope
tri-	three	tricycle, tripod
un-	not	unable, unhappy
uni-	one	unicorn, unison

Suffix	Meaning	Sample Words
-able, -ible	is, can be	climbable, gullible
-an	relating to	veteran, American
-ar, -er, -or	one, who	liar, teacher, editor
-er	more	smarter, luckier
-en	to make	fasten, weaken
-ess	one who (female)	waitress, actress
-est	most	closest, lightest
-ful	full of	joyful, fearful
-ish	relating to	bookish, selfish
-less	without	tireless, careless
-like	resembling	childlike, lifelike
-ly	resembling	motherly, sisterly
-ment	action, process	development, experiment
-ness	quality of	kindness, darkness

Form #29, page 1

Basic Phonics Rules

Listed below are some basic phonics rules to help students read and write better. This list is very short and by no means all-inclusive, as the English language is very complex.

Short Vowels Rules

- A short vowel sound corresponds to the sound in the following sample words: cat, pet, hit, hot, cut.

- Closed-Syllable Rule: If a vowel is located in the middle of a one syllable word (hat, sun, not), the vowel usually has a short sound.

- If there is one letter "e" in a word and the word ends with a consonant (help, next, spell), the "e" usually has the short sound.

- If a word ends in "ck," the sound of "k" is heard and the preceding vowel is short (chick).

Long Vowel Rules

- If two vowels are together in a word (coat, main, people, dream), the first vowel is usually long and the second vowel sound silent.

- If there is only one vowel at the end of a word, it is usually long (be, so, me).

- If a word has one vowel in the middle and ends with the letter "e" (cake, side, close), the middle vowel usually has a long sound and the final letter "e" is silent.

- Words with a double vowel "ee" (seen, green) usually take on the long "e" sound.

- If a word ends with an "ay" (day, play, say), the "a" takes on a long sound and the "y" is silent.

- If the letter "i" is followed by the letters "gh" (night, flight), the "i" takes on the long sound and the "gh" is silent.

Additional Rules

- Modified Vowels: If the medial vowel is followed by an r (cure, harm, firm), it becomes an "r" controlled vowel and usually has neither a long or short sound.

Form #29, page 2

Basic Phonics Rules

Additional Rules (continued)

- The "ie" (thief, pie, field) combination is frequently used, but this combination does not follow the consonant "c" (receive).

- The vowel combination of "ea" may take either a long (seat) or short (bread) sound.

- When certain consonants are positioned together in a word, they usually make one sound. Examples include church, there, white, bomb, telephone, knight, back, write, and gnat.

- If the consonant "c" is followed by one of the vowels "a," "o," or "u," the sound of "k" is usually heard. If the consonant "c" is followed by the vowels "a," "e," or "i," the sound of "s" is usually heard.

Form #30

Study Methods for Spelling

Read-and Spell Method

☐ Look at the word while it is read aloud.

☐ Read the word. Spell the word orally. Read the word again.

☐ Spell the word two times without looking at the model.

☐ Compare the word to the model.

Hear-and-Spell Method

☐ Observe while the word is written on a flashcard or the overhead.

☐ Read the word aloud. Listen while each letter is read aloud to you.

☐ Listen while each letter of the word is read aloud and repeat each letter.

☐ Spell the word aloud alone.

Cover-and-Write Method

☐ Read the word aloud from the model.

☐ Turn the model over (or cover it) and spell the word without looking.

☐ While viewing the word, write the word on a piece of paper.

☐ Compare the word to the model.

☐ If the word is correct, write the word three more times without looking at the model.

☐ Compare your word to the model. If it is correct, select another word to practice.

Form #31

Weekly Study Schedule

Time	Monday	Tuesday	Wednesday	Thursday	Friday
3:00-3:30					
3:30-4:00					
4:00-4:30					
4:30-5:00					
5:00-5:30					
5:30-6:00					
6:00-6:30					
6:30-7:00					
7:00-7:30					
7:30-8:00					
8:00-8:30					
8:30-9:00					
9:00-9:30					
9:30-10:00					

Block out the following time blocks on the schedule:
study time, after-school activities, athletics, dinner, and free time.

Form #32

Priority Assignment Sheet

Date	Priority Rating	Assignment	Time Allotment	Date Completed

Instructions: Use a pencil to fill in the following information. The priority list will change as the assignments are completed.

Date: Write in the date the assignment was given.

Priority Rating: Prioritize the assignment. The assignment listed as #1 should receive the highest priority.

Assignment: List the assignment and subject area.

Time Allotment: Estimate the amount of time needed to complete the assignment.

Date Completed: Place a check in the box and list the date the assignment is complete.

Form #33

Checklist– Materials to Bring Home

	Monday	Tuesday	Wednesday	Thursday	Friday
Assignment Book:	_____	_____	_____	_____	_____
Textbooks:					
English	_____	_____	_____	_____	_____
Math	_____	_____	_____	_____	_____
Social Studies	_____	_____	_____	_____	_____
English	_____	_____	_____	_____	_____
Science	_____	_____	_____	_____	_____
_____	_____	_____	_____	_____	_____
_____	_____	_____	_____	_____	_____
Supplies:					
Pencils/pens	_____	_____	_____	_____	_____
Colored pencils	_____	_____	_____	_____	_____
Markers	_____	_____	_____	_____	_____
Calculator	_____	_____	_____	_____	_____
_____	_____	_____	_____	_____	_____
_____	_____	_____	_____	_____	_____
Handouts:					
_____	_____	_____	_____	_____	_____
_____	_____	_____	_____	_____	_____
_____	_____	_____	_____	_____	_____
Study Guides:					
_____	_____	_____	_____	_____	_____
_____	_____	_____	_____	_____	_____
_____	_____	_____	_____	_____	_____
Graded Tests:					
_____	_____	_____	_____	_____	_____
_____	_____	_____	_____	_____	_____
_____	_____	_____	_____	_____	_____
Materials for Parent:					
_____	_____	_____	_____	_____	_____
_____	_____	_____	_____	_____	_____

Form #34

Common Abbreviations for Notetaking					
2	to	mph	miles per hour		
&	and	mth	month		
abv	above	n/t	next to		
aft	after	no	number		
amt	amount	nt	not		
ans	answer	opp	opposite		
assn	association	pop	population		
b/c	because	pp	pages		
bf	before	ppl	people		
bgn	begin	prob	problem		
bib	bibliography	sec	section		
biog	biography	sec	second		
blw	below	sq	square		
cap	capital	t/o	through out		
comp	complete	thru	through		
dept	department	tm	time		
dur	during	u	you		
ea	each	un	unit		
ed	edition	v	very		
etc	et cetera	w	with		
ex	example	w/o	without		
exer	exercise	wd	wide		
F	fahrenheit	wdth	width		
fin	finish	whn	when		
freq	frequency	wht	what		
gd	good	yr	year		
govt	government	mth	month		
hr	hour				
hsty	history				
ht	height				
illus	illustration				
imp	important				
inc	incomplete				
info	information				
lb	pound				
masc	masculine				
med	medium				
min	minute				
mny	many				

Add your own abbreviations to the list.

Form #35, page 1

"What do I do...?"

These questions may be used as discussion with the supervising teacher. You may also want to record some of the ideas here.

if a student refuses to do the required assignment?

if a student is asked to begin the work and refuses?

if a student rips up his assignment?

if a student continually blurts out answers during small group instruction?

if I ask a student to leave a small group and the student refuses?

if a student is instructed to clean up a mess he has created and refuses?

if a student talks back or responds in an inappropriate manner?

if a student gets angry and starts throwing objects in the classroom?

if a student runs in the hall, classroom, etc., and, after being asked, refuses to stop?

Form #35, page 2

"What do I do...?"

if a students runs away from me?

if a student continually swears quietly at his desk?

if a student hits and/or personally assaults another student?

if a student has an outburst in the classroom which disrupts the entire class?

if a student starts to use yell profanity directed to both the adults and the students?

if a student hits, pokes, and bothers other students in the classroom?

if a student continually arrives late to class?

if a student leaves the classroom without permission?

if a student leaves the classroom and does not return in the expected time frame?

Form #36

Behavior Change Plan

What happened? (list the incident that occurred)	What happened before the incident? (list the activity, subject, or any helpful information)	How did I respond?	What are some alternate responses if this situation reoccurs?
.			

Additional support needed or comments.

Form #37

Tally Sheet

Student	Date / Time	Observable Behavior
	Tally Space	
		Total
		Total
		Total
		Total

Tally Sheet

Student	Date / Time	Observable Behavior
	Tally Space	
		Total
		Total
		Total
		Total

Form #38

Sample Reinforcement Charts

Several types of reinforcement charts with suggestions for use are included below. The charts may be reproduced and used for multiple purposes. For this reason, headers have not been included on the charts.

Sample 1 – This chart may be used for homework assignments, work completion, behavior, etc.

Subject / Date	Monday	Tuesday	Wednesday	Thursday	Friday

Sample 2 – This chart may be used for behaviors that need to be documented frequently throughout the day.

Form #38, page 2

Picture Charts

For younger children, picture charts may be motivating. The following outlines may be used in several ways:

- Simple pictures may be cut apart into puzzle pieces. The student receives one puzzle piece as reinforcement. When the puzzle is complete, the student takes it home or turns it in for a reward.
- Simple dot-to-dot pictures may be created. For example the points of the star could be numbered from 1-10. The student connects the numbers and when the dot-to-dot is complete, the student receives a reward.

Form #38, page 3

The following charts may be used for students who require frequent feedback. List the target goal and at each check period, the student inserts a + or − in each box. The * indicates a reinforcement or reward if the goal has been met. In the first sample, the reinforcement would occur after two documented pluses. The following samples may be individualized for the student:

		*			*			*			*

Form #38, page 4

The following is a ladder chart. The student may color in the blocks and turn it in when the entire ladder is filled. In the sample rewards have been included randomly on the chart.

Sample:

	Step 8 You have reached your goal
	Step 7
	Step 6 Select a reward!
	Step 5
	Step 4
	Step 3 Five minutes free-time
	Step 2
	Step 1

	Step 8
	Step 7
	Step 6
	Step 5
	Step 4
	Step 3
	Step 2
	Step 1

Photocopy the following onto sheets of self-adhesive label paper. The student may cut them apart and stick the symbols onto the chart.

♥	♥	♥	♥	♥	♥	♥	♥	♥	♥	♥	♥
♣	♣	♣	♣	♣	♣	♣	♣	♣	♣	♣	♣
☺	☺	☺	☺	☺	☺	☺	☺	☺	☺	☺	☺
+	+	+	+	+	+	+	+	+	+	+	+

Form #39

Positive Reinforcement Phrases

Awesome!

Wow!

I discovered the secret to success!

Fantastic Day!

WAY TO GO!

Form #39, page 2

Positive Reinforcement Phrases

Super Star!

Congratulations!

I'm on a roll!

I had a great day today!

I am special!

Form #40

Point Sheet

Subject	Teacher	Number of Points Earned	Homework / Comment Section

Criteria

3 points_____

2 points_____

1 points_____

0 points_____

Appendix B

This Appendix includes the recommended resources listed in this publication and also additional resources for paraprofessionals. The majority of these publications are available directly from Peytral Publications. If you would like additional information, please call toll-free. 877-PEYTRAL (739-8725)

Alphabet Learning Center Activities Kit. Nancy Fetzer, Sandra Rief. Paramus, NJ. The Center for Applied Research ©2002

Collaborative Practices for Educators. Patty Lee. Minnetonka, MN. Peytral Publications, Inc. ©1999

Hands-On-Phonics Activities for Elementary Children. Karen Meyers Stangl. Paramus, NJ. The Center for Applied Research ©2000

Inclusion: Strategies for Working with Young Children. Lorraine O. Moore. Minnetonka, MN. Peytral Publications, Inc. ©2003

Let's Write! Cynthia M. Stowe. San Francisco, CA. Jossey-Bass. ©1997

Phonemic Awareness: Lessons, Activities and Games. Victoria Groves Scott. Peytral Publications, Inc. ©1999

"Phonemic Awareness: The Sounds of Reading" Staff Development Video. Victoria Groves Scott. Minnetonka, MN. Peytral Publications, Inc. ©2000

The Paraeducator's Guide to Instructional and Curricular Modifications. Wendy Dover. Manhattan, KS. The Master Teacher ©2001

The Paraprofessional's Guide to the Inclusive Classroom, Working as a Team. Mary Beth Doyle. Baltimore, MD. Paul H. Brookes Company ©2002

The Reading Teacher's Book of Lists. San Francisco, CA Jossey-Bass

The Reading Tutor's Handbook. Jeanne Shay Schumm, Ph.D., and Gerald Schumm, Jr. Minneapolis, MN. Free Spirit Publishing ©1999

Winning the Study Game – Learning How to Succeed in School. Minnetonka, MN. Peytral Publications, Inc. ©2003

Glossary

abstract thinking - ability to think in terms of ideas.

Adaptation - change which is made to the curriculum, instruction, environment, or material for an individual student.

ADD - see Attention Deficit Disorder

alternate assessments - an evaluation using various methods in place of traditional paper/pencil tests to assess a student's knowledge. Demonstrations, oral presentations, or projects are some examples.

Attention Deficit Disorder - a condition in which a student has difficulties in directing or maintaining attention to normal tasks involved in learning.

auditory blending - blending of sounds into words.

auditory discrimination - ability to hear differences and similarities in spoken words.

auditory memory - ability to recall information that is heard.

behavior - a relationship between a stimulus and a response.

behavior modification - the process which creates a change in the stimulus/response pattern.

cognitive ability - the ability to learn. Cognitive ability testing may also be referred to as intelligence testing.

collaboration - to work together towards a common goal.

configuration cues - the outline of a word in relation to the shape and length.

contract - a written agreement between teacher and student that outlines specific behaviors and consequences.

curricular modifications – changes to the actual curriculum. Curricular modifications are created by certified teaching staff.

discrimination - ability to differentiate between visual, auditory, tactual, or other sensory stimuli.

distractibility - attention that is easily moved away from the task.

expressive language – voice, gestures, and/or written expression.
fine motor - use of small muscle groups for specific tasks such as handwriting, cutting, or pasting.

hyperactivity - excessive activity in relation to others of the same age and in similar situations.

IEP - See Individualized Education Plan.

individual Education Plan - an individual program designed for a student who qualifies for special education services.

impulsivity - acting or speaking out without considering the consequences.

inclusion paraprofessional - a person who works with a specific group of students in an inclusive classroom.

inclusive education pupil paraprofessional - a person who is assigned to support a specific student. The assistant is written into the IEP.

inclusive schooling - a school setting in which students receive their educational instruction within the classroom setting for the entire or a substantial portion of their school day.

least restrictive environment - a term requiring that, to the greatest possible extent, students with disabilities are educated with their nondisabled peers.

modifications - adaptations made in the curriculum, presentation method, or the environment to provide support for an individual student

memory - recall of visual, auditory, and or tactile stimuli.

mnemonics - visual or word-related aids that facilitate retrieval of information.

parallel activity - an assignment in which the outcome is similar but the materials used to reach the outcome may be entirely different.

previewing - reading, listening to, or viewing the selection before instruction or a test.

readiness - physical, mental, and emotional preparedness for a learning activity.

short attention span - inability to pay attention to something for a long period of time compared to others of the same age.

supplemental teaching - provisions provided to the student in the form of reteaching, reinforcement and/or alternate curriculum when needed.

supportive teaching - modifications made to the classroom curriculum or the environment by the special education teacher or paraprofessional which will allow the student to experience success in the general education setting.

sound symbol - relationship between the printed form of a letter and the sound.

team teaching - two or more teachers working together to develop, plan, and teach a lesson.

visual discrimination - ability to perceive likenesses and differences in pictures, words, and symbols.

Notes

Notes

Notes

Notes

Notes

Notes

Notes

Notes

CORWIN PRESS

The Corwin Press logo—a raven striding across an open book—represents the union of courage and learning. Corwin Press is committed to improving education for all learners by publishing books and other professional development resources for those serving the field of PreK–12 education. By providing practical, hands-on materials, Corwin Press continues to carry out the promise of its motto: **"Helping Educators Do Their Work Better."**